SEXUAL RECOVERY

Everywoman's Guide
Through Sexual Co-dependency

Gina Ogden, Ph.D.

Health Communications, Inc.
Deerfield Beach, Florida

Gina Ogden, Ph.D.
Cambridge, Massachusetts

Library of Congress Cataloging-in-Publication Data

Ogden, Gina.
Sexual Recovery
    Everywoman's guide through sexual co-dependency/Gina Ogden.
    p.   cm.
    Includes bibliographical references.
    ISBN 1-55874-068-6
    1. Co-dependents — Sexual behaviors. 2. Sexual addiction.
3. Women — Mental health.   I. Title.
RC569.5.C63037   1990   90-34982
616.85'83 — dc20   CIP

Publisher: Health Communications, Inc.
            3201 S.W. 15th Street
            Deerfield Beach, Florida 33442

Cover design by Iris T. Slones

DEDICATION

For Jo, who continues to help me step over the cracks in the yellow brick road.

If only I could walk into your eyes and shut the lids behind me and leave all the world outside.

Sheilah Graham

Allowing your life to be taken over by someone else is like letting the waiter eat your dinner.

Vernon Howard

CONTENTS

Wholeness; Steps To Sexual Wholeness; Setting The
Stage For Sexual Wholeness.

❧ ACKNOWLEDGMENTS ❧

Deep thanks to the clients who have opened up their hearts and their lives to me in the last 15 years. They taught me not only about the agonies of sexual co-dependency but also about the struggle back to freedom and sexual integration. In particular, I want to thank the ACoA Special Interest Group for their enthusiasm for this project. It wouldn't exist without them.

Deep thanks also to Jo-Ann Krestan and Claudia Bepko for longtime guidance on the spirit of recovery.

Two colleagues have been particularly helpful in reviewing this manuscript. I am grateful to Dr. Margery Noel for her clinical expertise and to Dr. Beverly Whipple for updating the scientific details.

Examples in this book are based on true stories but names and details have been changed to protect the identities of those concerned.

INTRODUCTION

Women and children are particularly open to being hurt by sex. They are victims of incest, rape, battering, pornography and prostitution. If this were not enough, they also encounter problems with the sexual double standard, taboos about sexual behavior and restrictions on birth control. In addition there are the medical problems that can be associated with sexual behavior, the ravages of herpes and chlamydia and the lethal dangers of AIDS (Acquired Immune Deficiency Syndrome). Last but not least are the complications introduced by drug and alcohol abuse.

These sexual horrors are built into our culture. Children and women are routinely treated in addictive, assaultive ways in this world. The exact scenario may change from generation to generation but the result is always the same: Sex can hurt women no matter what their age, race or economic situation. It's hard for some women to develop a secure idea of what personal safety means, let alone sexual safety.

Given such a situation, why do women risk having sexual relationships? Because along with the potential for fear and pain, sex has the potential to feel downright wonderful. And in addition to pleasure, sex can be a powerful force for personal recovery from all sorts of addictions and addictive relationships. Sexual pleasure and satisfaction offer increased energy, relaxation, integration and connection with a partner.

It is my clinical experience that making love pleasurably and sanely is possible even in a dangerous world. It's even possible after the heartbreak of growing up in an alcoholic home or after the devastation of incest or any of the other forms of sexual abuse.

How can women detox their sexual relationships and reclaim the pleasure that is their birthright? That is the story of this book.

❊| ONE |❊

Sexual Co-dependency And
How It Develops

Sex is supposed to be a pleasure. But for women it is too often connected with violence, coercion or disease. Then sex becomes toxic. It hurts, disgusts and terrifies.

Many women live in chronic fear of sex and of their own sexual feelings. They act out this fear through co-dependencies in the bedroom. Some are locked into a dysfunctional two-step with toxic partners, others generate toxicity themselves. Some do both:

- **Bonnie** doesn't know how to take care of herself. She leaves herself open to unsafe partners and unsafe sex.
- **Denise** depends entirely on her partner's sexual response for her good feelings. When her partner isn't satisfied she feels like a failure.
- **Dianne** has never been able to come to orgasm, no matter how much her partner wants her to. When her partner doesn't satisfy her, Dianne feels like a failure. At times she feels suicidally lonely.

- **Rose** says she can't stop coming to orgasm or thinking about it — and that's a problem because she spends so much time in bed that she can't keep up with her studies. As a result her scholarship for law school is in jeopardy. She feels as if her whole life is careening out of control.

Each of these women has developed an unsatisfying pattern of relationship as a defense against the fear and pain she connects with sex. Each of these women has become sexually co-dependent.

When sex doesn't work, what is supposed to lead to satisfaction ends up in frustration. What is supposed to flow spontaneously becomes rigid and driven. Sexual unhappiness may dictate how you organize your life. Since sexuality is an integral part of yourself — of your body, mind, heart and soul — your personal serenity may twirl into a tailspin.

The effects can be devastating, especially if it's not okay for you to talk about what's going on — which it usually isn't. Your partner may be part of the problem, or anyway, too close to the situation. Your children are inappropriate to use as confidantes. Your friends may get too embarrassed or too involved. Your co-workers might take it as a come-on. Besides, sex is something women in this culture are taught not to talk about.

When sex doesn't work, what do most women do?

Grin and bear it. Wallow in self-pity. Sink into denial. Break up their relationships. Enter into new relationships over and over again.

There is another choice: learning to make love sanely. This involves, first of all, fully understanding and accepting what the problems are. Not only the physical problems but the emotional and relational ones — the problems of sexual co-dependency. Only then is it possible to move toward making sex a beneficial part of your personal recovery; something that feels safe and right while it is happening and that leaves you with a sense of well-being for a long time afterwards.

Let's start by listening to three women, Barbara, Joyce and Rebecca. Like many women today, they are actively recovering from addictive behaviors but they're still in the dark about sex — the kind of intimate sex that feels like making *love*.

Barbara 1: Bar-Hopping Sex

I feel like a sexual freak.

When I look back on my drinking and drugging days I shudder. I didn't mind picking up somebody different every night. I ended up with a lot of self-loathing, a couple of broken ribs and a case of herpes.

Then, when I was getting sober, I got the message that this was pretty sick behavior, not to mention being dangerous. So I quit. I quit bar-hopping and I quit sex. That was four years ago. And frankly I'm just as terrified of having sex right now as I am of taking another drink.

But I want to be in a relationship. The kind of relationship where you live together and share your life. Well that includes sex, doesn't it?

I don't want the kind of sex where you trance out and wake up four days later not knowing who's in bed next to you. I want to learn to make love without blowing my mind.

Joyce 1: Ravages Of Sexual Abuse

Joyce has lived alone from the minute she could support herself. In all her adult life, she has never had sex and has never even been out on a date. She was three when the first of her "stepfathers" began incesting her and five when she remembers sitting on the stairs watching the Saturday night poker crowd systematically gang-raping her mother on the kitchen table. There are many years of her childhood that Joyce cannot remember at all . . .

. . . and I'm grateful for not remembering. Why would I want to go back and try to recreate all that? What I can remember is bad enough.

I can honestly say I hate men. Or at least I don't trust them. Why should I? I hate them for what they did to me. I hate them for what they did to my mother. But even more, I resent them for being untrustworthy. In spite of this I don't like living all alone.

I want someone to love. I want a family. I guess you'd say I want
to be normal.

But I don't know how to get close. I don't have a close friend,
never mind a lover. I don't have a dog, a cat or a bird. I don't even
know where to begin.

Rebecca 1: Sober Without Sexual Is Not Enough

Rebecca is a social worker, an Adult Daughter of alcoholic
parents, with six years in 12-Step programs. Unlike Barbara or
Joyce, she is in a long-standing, monogamous partnership —
with a woman. She identifies this partnership as "grossly co-
dependent" and she is working hard to get a handle on it.

The piece of the puzzle I'm having the most trouble figuring
out is the sexual piece. We're certainly passionate but our lovemaking is wild, obsessive, insane. We're hooked to each other and
we make each other miserable as often as we make each other
happy. I know I'm supposed to have the answers inside me — and
honestly I've been searching. But I can tell you, I think I just don't
have a full library.

Rebecca's story could go on and on. She could talk about
her loneliness within her partnership, even during sex; about
how she feels even more isolated than some of her friends
feel without any partner at all.

She could relate how, when she feels insecure, she turns
into a sexual hemophiliac, hemorrhaging attention on her
partner, whether her partner wants it or not.

She could catalogue how her hungry, overloyal, overcon-
trolling, gullible, blaming, roller-coaster self makes chaos out
of lovemaking. How, particularly because she is a woman and
a lesbian, she has problems finding meaningful role models
for stable, assertive sex.

She could also tell us how sensitive she is and how fun-
loving and how orgasmically responsive. Above all, she
could tell us how much she wants to learn how to make
love, not trouble.

Like many women in recovery, Rebecca has learned that sober without sexual is not enough. Addictions educators are discovering that relapses into addictive behaviors are often due to unresolved sexual issues. In addition, the age of AIDS has made it imperative that women learn to deal openly and creatively with sexual issues. Particularly for women who can't say No, learning assertive options for sexual expression could spell the difference between life and death.

In the course of all her searching, Rebecca has learned a lesson that is true for thousands of women in recovery: Sexual function does not happen just because you work a 12-Step program. Sober does not necessarily mean sexual (and I invite you to define sober in any way you choose). In fact, sex may actually get worse as women begin feeling more in control of the rest of their lives. Making love *insanely* may feel better at first than making love *sanely* — and you'll hear lots more about this paradox as you continue to read this book.

Rebecca has yet to learn that sexual recovery can be an important and joyful part of her total recovery. This book is written as a gentle guide for Rebecca, Joyce, Barbara and for others who are ready to incorporate fully responsive and responsible sexuality into their personal growth and into their relationships.

Let's start with a common understanding of terms.

What Is Sexual Co-dependency?

> If only I could walk into your eyes and close the lids behind me
> and leave all the world outside . . .

Sheilah Graham wrote this to F. Scott Fitzgerald in the post-Prohibition 1930s and countless women in my clinical practice have responded to it with a wistful sigh — a nostalgic kind of longing:

> It's so romantic to think of losing yourself forever in a lover's eyes. It's so comforting to imagine that you never have to deal with the world alone again. I wish someday I could have the experience of being loved like that.

Walking into someone's eyes and shutting the lids behind you is a graphic image of one kind of sexual co-dependency — a kind called fusing or merging, where you lose your boundaries and don't know where you end and someone else begins.

There are other ways co-dependency can play itself out in a relationship, too. Over the years I've talked with hundreds of co-dependent couples in therapy:

- Fused couples, like Sheilah Graham and F. Scott Fitzgerald.
- Distant couples, whose mating dance keeps them at arm's length.
- Hot and cold couples, where one wants sex and the other doesn't.

It doesn't seem to matter whether these couples are heterosexual or lesbian, old faithfuls or newly in love. It doesn't matter whether they are recovering substance abusers or nonusers their whole lives long. They have come into my office at odds with one another because the sex doesn't work. Through them, I've arrived at a working definition of sexual co-dependency for women.

Sexual co-dependency is a painful pattern of lovemaking in which one's attitudes and behaviors are habitually determined by someone else.

It means you consistently rely on somebody else to provide you with your sense of sexual self-worth. You have no way to tap into your inner center of sexual wisdom and serenity.

It means you have developed compulsively unrewarding patterns of sexual behavior at any or all phases of your sexual relationship, from attraction to commitment, from arousal to orgasm.

It means your mating dance is an out-of-control shuffle between manipulating a partner and being manipulated.

It means you organize your sexual encounters around sabotage rather than satisfaction. You may consciously or unconsciously pick a partner who won't or can't meet you — even halfway.

In sexual co-dependency, your sexual expectations are based on fantasy rather than actual experience. One or both of the following is likely to be true for you:

1) You expect your partner to meet your sexual needs even though he or she has hardly ever come through for you.
2) You expect your partner *not* to meet your needs even though he or she consistently has (or does) come through for you.

To spell this out: There are gaps in your sexual frame of reference — you don't know what sexually "normal" is. You build sexual trust on unfounded hopes. You build sexual distrust on old emotional tapes. You develop bedroom roles on assumptions rather than on what is actually happening in the present. You develop personality traits that ensure that sexual intimacy is impossible. You use sex to fill needs that could be filled more appropriately in other ways.

You may even shy away from sex when it might bring warmth and joy to your life.

Before you jump to conclusions and start diagnosing yourself, and perhaps a few other people you know, be aware that having great expectations and playing bedroom roles once in a while or for fun doesn't make you sexually co-dependent. Nor does having information gaps. Nor does being in love, or counting on a partner for your sexual delight and satisfaction.

How Do You Know If You're Sexually Co-dependent?

Sexual co-dependency involves a whole pattern of negative sexual relationship. The tipoffs are these:

1. Your sexual encounters are unsatisfying to you. You feel disconnected or fragmented. Your feelings are unplugged from one another, both in your sexual encounters and also in the rest of your life.
2. You're unaware of your expectations or of the bedroom roles you play. If you are aware, you feel as if you're running a collision course with them. You don't know

how to stop even when you want to. You may not know
any other ways to behave in the bedroom.

3. These expectations and roles are familiar. They fit you
   like your favorite old sneakers. You've played them for
   a long time and you're good at them. Sexual co-dependency doesn't happen overnight and it is not a one- or
   two-shot deal.

4. Although these expectations and roles are yours, you're
   not the only one in the game. Your partner plays an
   integral part and may have a complementary set of expectations and roles that dovetails with yours. As a stu-
   dent in one of my classes puts it: "It takes two to tangle."

5. You may have these disconnections and expectations
   and play these roles with one partner and not another.

6. These disconnections, expectations and roles are tied
   to old ones you learned in order to survive earlier
   stresses in your life. To think about changing them
   now may feel terrifying because they're part of your
   whole defense system.

Recognizing co-dependency as your pattern of lovemaking
may be depressing because it may seem that there is no end
in sight. Indeed co-dependency is often described as a disease,
an addiction, like alcoholism and drug abuse — entirely negative, with no saving graces.

Please take heart, however, and read on. I've found in my
clinical work that among the dysfunctional patterns of sexual
co-dependency lurk some extremely positive patterns that can
enhance sexual function and growth. Moreover, developing
these patterns involves skills that can be translated into personal connection. The good news will come later though.
Let's start the story at its negative beginnings.

How Do Women Become Sexually Co-dependent?

Where, when and how do women develop out-of-control
reliances on their partners and learn to play unrewarding
bedroom roles? Sexual co-dependency has three roots:

1. Post-Traumatic Stress
2. Skewed psychosexual development
3. Sex-negative, woman-negative cultural influences

These are pieces of growing up that are common to all children in our culture, especially to girls. If you think of these roots as the legs of a triangle, you can find the size and shape of your individual sexual co-dependency. Figure 1.1 shows the basic sexual co-dependency triangle.

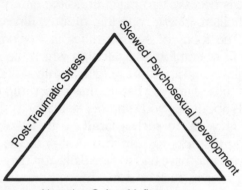

Negative Cultural Influences

Figure 1.1. Roots Of Sexual Co-dependency.

Each woman's experience is different, so post-traumatic stress, skewed psychosexual development and negative cultural influences will vary from woman to woman and may also vary in the course of a lifetime. At times, your sexual co-dependency triangle may blow up into a huge balloon that affects your life in overwhelming ways. On the other hand, it may dwindle to the size of a peanut so that you don't even notice it.

Here's a description of each one of these roots.

Post-Traumatic Roots Of Sexual Co-dependency

At this writing, researchers believe that co-dependency is learned, not inherited. There's no evidence that it begins in the womb, although the stunning recent studies on alcohol and crack-addicted babies indicate that physiological addiction can begin there.

Patterns of co-dependency can, and often do, begin early on in life to help children survive trauma, in particular, the trauma of family dynamics that are incompatible with a healthy childhood. Such dynamics include the coercions and self-flagellations necessary to maintain as the family focus issues like alcoholism, incest, battering, disaster, illness or fanatical religion. The focus of such families is *not* on creating an atmosphere of comfort and safety in which the children can learn positive, age-appropriate relationship skills.

Any of these family dynamics has direct impact on how a child feels about her body and her sexuality as she grows up.

If you grew up in such a family, you probably learned a mixed bag of tricks to help you deal with the stresses and traumas you may have had to face daily. You may have learned negative patterns, such as defensive withdrawal and eventual substance abuse. You may have learned positive coping patterns, such as household skills and efficient management. Also you may have learned patterns that are a mixed blessing to you now, such as the ability to please, placate and entertain or the capacity for hard work. Inevitably, if you grew up in one of these families, you learned to invalidate your own feelings.

Because sex has to do with relationships, these patterns that you learned affected your sexual development.

As you reached adulthood, your stress-response patterns tended to remain, unless you made a conscious effort to change them. Whether your learned responses to stress were positive, negative, or ambiguous, you may have continued to behave as if you were responding to stress even once the stresses were no longer there.

Effects Of Stress-Response Patterns

In your present life, you may feel as if you are living on the edge. You may be alternately anxious and depressed. You may experience flashbacks to traumatic events. You may have to struggle to maintain an emotional balance, because if your current stresses become too great, you fear you may crack wide open, lose control and allow all the feelings from those early stresses to come tumbling out.

If this is true for you, you may find yourself choosing a mate or a life situation that protects you from stress. That is, you have become to some degree compulsively dependent on something or someone outside yourself to insulate you from the world. You may retreat from people, avoid sex and become a hermit, or you may allow a partner to make your decisions. You play by the rules. You may be bored to distraction but you feel relatively safe this way. Your sex may be safe, too, but you experience it as incredibly dull, maybe even nonexistent.

On the other hand, the absence of stress may cause you to become so anxious, uncomfortable or *dis*-stressed that you choose a mate or slip into a life situation to create emergencies you can respond to. You become an ambulance squad volunteer or hook up with an alcoholic or "forget" to balance your checkbook. Your sex is likely to be high risk, too.

These are highly simplified glimpses of a much more complex picture but they should be enough to illustrate the point. If you recognize yourself in these scenarios, then you have become chronically addicted to stress. That is, you have become to some degree compulsively dependent on a partner or situation to keep the stress level high enough to keep your anxiety level in control. If the stress is removed, you may find that you fall apart like a two-dollar suit — and you live in constant fear of falling apart, which creates internal stress of its own.

In this chronic sense, then, co-dependency is a kind of time bomb or emotional jet lag. To describe the symptoms, psychologists have coined the term Post-Traumatic Stress Disorder (PTSD). In this construct, Adult Children of stress and trauma exhibit the same symptoms as shell-shocked veterans of war. The Adult Child or the Vietnam vet may be alert with guerrilla survival skills as long as the enemy is at their throats but once the stresses are removed or if new, unpredictable stresses appear, the emotion has a chance to surface. That's when they risk going berserk and shooting up the hometown fast food joint.

To summarize, the post-traumatic roots of sexual co-dependency have the following characteristics:

- They are learned.
- They often begin early as survival mechanisms.
- They may generate positive patterns as well as negative ones.
- They always invalidate your sense of self.
- They tend to remain even when your situation changes.
- They may create phobic avoidance of stress.
- They may create compulsive dependencies on more stress.

Julia 1: Post-Traumatic Sex

How does sexual co-dependency grow out of post-traumatic stress? Julia's story is an example. Persistently yelled at by her alcoholic mother while she was a child, Julia was also raped by an uncle when she was 13. Julia was a family hero, a perfect child and perfect wife, who was able to swallow her reactions to these traumatic stresses until she was raped again — this time by her husband just after their child was born.

> I still had the stitches from my episiotomy and I thought he was going to split me in two. He said, "We have to start having sex sometime and it might as well be right now." He wouldn't hear me say no. He wouldn't stop even though I screamed and almost passed out from the pain. He never said he was sorry afterwards, even though he could see the blood on the sheets.

When I first saw Julia in therapy, she was sexually numb. She had no desire for physical pleasure except nursing her baby, which she found to be a great comfort. She avoided any kind of touch from her husband and had lost the desire and ability to experience orgasm. Although she was physically exhausted from being a new mother, she had trouble falling asleep and she regularly woke at night screaming. At this point Julia could no longer control her memories:

> When I close my eyes, all I can see is how my uncle looked at me when he asked me to pull my panties down. His eyes were small and kind of glittery as if they were on fire. I don't know why I'm remembering all this now. That was 15 years ago. My situation is entirely different now.

Although Julia was resisting her husband's sexual advances, she also felt guilty that she was depriving him of what he wanted — sex. She had become more and more compliant in other areas of their life since the post-partum rape.

> I'm so afraid he'll leave me. There's no way I could ever make it on my own, especially with the baby. And I feel so awful that I'm not a good wife to him anymore. I try to make it up to him by making sure everything in the house is nice for him. I only wish I could feel more attracted to him.

Julia's story of unresolved post-traumatic stress leads into the next leg of the sexual co-dependency triangle — skewed psychosexual development. Let's link the development of co-dependency with the development of your sexuality.

Psychosexual Roots Of Sexual Co-dependency

Sexual function is not something that begins on your wedding night, when you are supposed to magically become knowledgeable, responsive and multiorgasmic. And it's not something that begins suddenly at puberty, when you can no longer hide the fact that you're a woman — that is, when you begin to sprout breasts and pubic hair and to menstruate for the first time (or get afflicted with the curse, if that's what you learned to call it). Nor does it start when you have your first crush, your first genital thrill or when you masturbate for the first time.

Your sexuality doesn't suddenly begin at these times any more than it suddenly ends with menopause — or with divorce or with drugs, alcohol, gambling, shopping, eating, obsessing, raging or any other life event you care to name.

The roots of sexual function begin even before birth, when you are in your mother's uterus — the most intimate you will ever be with anyone. Your sexual serenity (or lack of it) may be linked with how your mother felt when she was pregnant with you and how she took care of herself.

What was *her* self-image like? How did she feel about being pregnant with you? Did she want you? Was she able to nourish her body (and yours) or did she drink, smoke or do drugs? Did she have the emotional and economic support to be sending you calm and loving messages as you developed inside her or did she have to make her own way in a hostile world, perhaps enduring psychological or physical brutality?

Birth And Beyond

However your sexuality was prenatally influenced, your psychosexual development began in earnest as soon as you were born and even during your birthing experience.

- Were you welcomed gently into the world?
- As an infant and growing toddler were you nursed, cuddled, nurtured and encouraged to explore yourself and your sensuous responses to the world?
- Did your parents or other caregivers model a vibrant and loving adult relationship for you as you got older?

If so, chances are you began to move along the developmental stages into appropriate, satisfying expressions of your sexual being — that is, unless somewhere along the line you experienced incest, rape, harassment, sexism, religious prohibition or some other trauma that interrupted your positive psychosexual development.

The origins of your sexual co-dependency can be traced back to your birth, too, and to your birth process.

- Was your birth rushed, rough, noisy, full of bright lights, anxiety or medication?
- Did you require intrusive medical procedures like a Caesarean section, surgery or isolation?

With your very first breaths you may have had to develop defensive attitudes about your body. Your upbringing may also have affected the development of sexual co-dependency. If you were unwanted, neglected, battered, invaded or incested or if you were given negative or double messages about sex — all of these factors affected how you learned to relate sensually and sexually to yourself and others. Chances are you are experiencing emotional jet lag and are having trouble making love sanely now.

To put this into perspective so far: How many women do you know whose psychosexual development has been entirely positive from the moment of birth? I haven't yet met a woman whose sexual road was entirely smooth, even if she had the most loving and caring of parents. In particular those of us who grew up in homes where there were addictive dynamics, may have found the path to sexual growth extremely rocky.

Add the story of how you develop sexually to how your co-dependency develops, and you can begin to picture the degree of your sexual co-dependency. As you can imagine, most of us don't grow up knowing how to make love safely, satisfyingly and intimately. This is something we have to learn.

To summarize, the psychosexual roots of sexual co-dependency have the following characteristics:

- They may begin before birth and may be affected by your birthing experience.
- They grow with negative or nonexistent sex education.
- They grow with trauma or negative attitudes you experienced.
- They invalidate your sense of self.
- They tend to remain even when your situation changes.

- They may create phobic avoidance of sex.
- They may create compulsive dependencies on sex.

There is also the third leg of the triangle that needs to be factored into your sexual co-dependency equation. That is, society: the messages we get from the culture about being women and about being sexual.

Cultural Roots Of Sexual Co-dependency

Women are Adult Children of Stress just from being born into this society. Even if parents do everything right, there are influences in the culture that create dependent sexual patterns for women. No girl child escapes them. These range from our national embarrassment about sex (men are supposed to have all the answers) to the sexual degradation and terrorism of women in the media and in real life.

The culture has always given men the right to sexually appropriate women. In feudal days, this was spelled out in language everyone could understand. It was called *droit du seigneur* — the right of the lord of the manor. Among the rights of the feudal lord was to have intercourse with any of his female serfs on her wedding night or, in actual practice, on any occasion he chose.

While *droit du seigneur* is no longer on the law books, there is a fallout that remains today — a kind of cultural PTSD. Most women grow up with the idea, and the fear, that they are "fair game" for men. This cultural fallout not only victimizes and pressures women, it also forces men into a defensive position. This is particularly hard on those men who are advocates of sexual equality and really do think about a woman's well-being.

The Eve Syndrome

Women are especially open to sexual abuse if they are "different" — that is, if they do not conform to the American standard of being white, able-bodied, college-educated, middle class, Judeo-Christian and heterosexual. These women may develop co-dependent sexual attitudes as a defense against sexist, classist or racist *droit du seigneur* attitudes.

Whether you're "different" or not, you may have been expected to play good girl, subordinate, caretaker roles throughout your life. In fact, your parents may have trained you to play such roles out of concern for your well-being. Gender-based role-playing permeates this culture at every level, from home to workplace. It affects women even when their primary relationships are basically healthy. And it can skew what goes on in the bedroom — even if your partner is a woman.

Look at the widespread blaming of women for wanting knowledge, personal growth and sexual awareness. This is what I call the *Eve Syndrome* — a cultural habit that says it's all Eve's fault that Paradise didn't work out. What an uppity woman for wanting more than the day-to-day ho-hum of a male-dominated Eden.

Even on the brink of the 21st century, Good Girls still create no waves. Good Women create no sexual pressures for men. They certainly don't go around looking for sexual pleasure. They stay docile in the missionary position, faking orgasm if necessary, to keep their mates secure in the illusion that they are lovers from Paradise. And also — this cannot be emphasized too highly — to keep themselves from being put down, beaten, abandoned and cut off from economic resources.

Above all, Good Girls and Good Women are not supposed to take care of their own sexual needs. My clinical experience tells me that even women who are assertive in other areas of their lives can fall into a co-dependency trap of servicing their sexual partners without adequate return. This is sexual co-dependency in full flower. It colors women's responses and satisfaction in all phases of sexual relationship — attraction, excitement, seduction, romance, commitment, love and intimacy.

Sexual co-dependency causes women to feel unsatisfied during their sexual encounters. More importantly, they may feel disconnected — disconnected sexually, and also disconnected in the rest of their lives. They may sometimes feel crazy, like Joyce, who was abused so early in her life. Because of the cultural denial about women's sexuality, women don't have permission to talk about the pain, let alone talk about what to do about it.

Women get blamed for the trouble in Paradise. But women also blame themselves, and they blame their mates. This blame game creates personality problems and relationship problems.

Everyone's story has its own individual quirks about how sexual co-dependency develops. So in piecing together your own story and in finding the size and shape of your sexual co-dependency, it's important to factor in the cultural influences along with your family influences.

To summarize, the cultural roots of sexual co-dependency have the following characteristics:

- No woman escapes them.
- They are more pronounced for women who are "different."
- They invalidate your sense of self.
- They remain even when your primary relationship is equal.
- They may create Good Girl/Bad Girl role-playing.
- They may create sexual blame and self-blame.
- They may create compulsive dependencies on a sexual partner.

⚜ TWO ⚜

Your Emotional Armor Against Pain — And Pleasure

When a country is attacked, it throws up defenses — and that's exactly what you do in the face of sex that hurts or brings up memories of hurt. Building defensive structures under attack is a healthy, predictable reaction of your body, mind, emotions and spirit. If the hurt is intense, you may develop a suit of armor that rivals Joan of Arc's.

The problem with personal armor is that it protects you from more than pain. It also protects you from feeling pleasure. It immobilizes you. Have you ever watched old Robin Hood movies in which unhorsed knights sprawl spluttering in mudpuddles? Armor can trap you inside as well as keep others out and it's not always easy to take your armor off once you get it on. You may have worn it so long that it functions like a second skin.

So imagine trying to make love in full armor — chest and back plates, pointed visor, arms and legs creaking with hinges, metal scales on your fingers and double chain mail shielding every other inch. Do you get the picture?

If you want to complicate matters, imagine your partner is

also in a suit of armor. Lovemaking between two Adult Children may not feel like a way to enjoy pleasure and satisfaction on a Sunday afternoon. It may feel more like a stalemate.

For instance, the woman who desperately wants more sex but who consistently picks fights with her partner the minute they get to bed might as well be behind a shield of steel and leather, for she is keeping sex at bay like a seasoned warrior.

For some examples of armor and how it can create its own problems, let's return to the women whose stories opened the book. As we explore the complex tapestry of their backgrounds, we see addiction, abuse, abandonment, deprivation, betrayal, humiliation. We can see why their defenses were so necessary. How else were they to survive the trauma, misogyny and negative messages about sex they grew up with? We can also begin to see how the armor that has saved their lives in the past is contributing now to their sexual dysfunction.

Joyce 2: A Chink In Her Armor

Joyce originally developed her armor to remove herself from the repeated episodes of forced oral sex with her stepfather and also to erase the scene of her stepfather and five poker-playing buddies holding her mother down on the kitchen table while they took turns raping her.

The armor Joyce carried into adult life was numbness — in particular, sexual anesthesia and intimacy anesthesia. Self-anesthetized, she protected herself from intolerable events — and memories of intolerable events — by having no feelings, no wants, no needs, by being someplace else, mentally and emotionally.

> I learned to space out. To not be there. If I wasn't there, I couldn't feel anything, it wasn't happening.

For many years, she maintained her armor quite consciously, steering clear of any relationship that seemed as if it could possibly become close.

On her 30th birthday, however, she woke up too depressed to go to work. Later that year she joined an Adult Children of Alcoholics (ACoA) group and eventually entered therapy. She began to see some healthy relationships around her and to wish she could have some of her own. Deep inside, she could feel the loss of closeness and she could feel the longing for it. But she still couldn't feel the closeness itself. In particular what she couldn't feel was sexual desire and excitement.

> You can't suddenly turn your feelings on. It's as if I threw the master switch a whole lot of years ago and have lost the key. It isn't just a question of trying harder or "breathing into it." It just doesn't compute with me. I don't feel close with myself; how can I feel close with another person? I can't even imagine what happy sexual feelings must be like. It must be like magic to know — a kind of sorcery, like being able to read music or Japanese. To me it all seems like chicken tracks.

To add to Joyce's distress, nowhere in her life outside groups and therapy had she received reinforcement that her armor had been a normal mechanism for her survival. Her life reached a crisis when a fellow worker called her a frigid old maid.

> I believed him. I could have shriveled up and died. I felt so inadequate, so abnormal, so bad.

Sad to say, this part of Joyce's story is all too common for women.

Sexually armored women may have to endure secondary attacks that cause them to reinforce their armor.

Attacks That Reinforce Armor

Attacks, or seeming attacks, on women's sexual selves can come not only from relative outsiders but from important people in their lives. Often they come from the very people who could help women open up, namely their partners and their doctors. An attack can come from a husband who threatens punishment or forced sex or finding another woman who'll give him all the sex he wants — and feels he *deserves*.

Or an attack can come from a gynecologist, who, instead of listening with understanding, quotes from the Book — the medical Book that catalogues individual pathologies, among them the pathology of women who are not sexually desirous, inviting, compliant or "attractive."

Attacks can also come from the media. Read the covers of women's magazines as you check out of the supermarket. Watch television ads. Look everywhere. Headlines will yell at you:

JUST SAY YES TO SEXY!

But our culture is oblivious to the fact that most women need to feel safe to feel sexy.

Joyce was called a frigid old maid because she didn't flirt, didn't play the dating game — because she avoided sex. Blaming serves only to strengthen personal armor, until some women have such good defenses they feel as if they are trapped in an invincible tower, like Rapunzel.

Joyce's doctor didn't improve her situation when Joyce visited him.

> I remember when my family doctor began to make jokes about my loosening up and enjoying it. He'd known me all my life. I thought I could trust him with my problem. When I opened up to him, he said, "You're an attractive woman. I could fall for you myself. Why don't you just let down your hair and live a little?"
>
> His back was turned to me when he said that. He sort of tossed it over his shoulder. He didn't even look me in the eyes. Thank heavens. Because if he'd seen what happened inside me in those few moments, he'd probably have called the police. I felt as if I was in one of those horror movies — where the hero turns into a giant fly or a werewolf. Only this was all happening inside me. My hands were turning into claws and my face was all gnarled and warty. But it was all inside. On the outside was a thick wall. A thick smiling wall that was the other me.

What was happening inside Joyce was not as bizarre as it sounds. In fact, it was a normal response and a predictable one. Her doctor's remarks may have been well-meaning banter on his part (let's give him the benefit of the doubt) but they were personal and sexual — just when Joyce had opened a chink in her armor and had allowed herself to be vulnerable. She experienced the remarks as an attack — a rape of her person that served to restimulate traumatic memories of earlier and sometimes "well-meaning" rapes by family and family friends, against which she had had no defense.

Joyce's monstrous transformation was not a cognitive memory that she could call up at will. It was not even a flashback in a literal sense. But it was a memory — a memory of feelings long stored in the body; in the cells, organs, muscles and bones. The body memory that Joyce experienced involved the feelings that were so overwhelming when she was a little girl — the guilt, shame, rage and grief that she had spent her whole life armoring herself against ever having to feel again.

Flashbacks

Was her "hallucination" the raving of a deranged brain or was it a step toward sexual health, a flood of feelings organizing themselves into an image she could recognize and remember on a cognitive level?

To answer this question for yourself, consider that denial and flashbacks can be part of the normal way of life for women who have grown up with trauma. They can also be part of normalizing life. Such armor is basically life-saving even though it may be diagnosable by therapists as sexual dysfunction, gender confusion, hallucinations, dissociative behavior and suicidal ideation.

In my practice I've found that it's seldom helpful to use pathological labels for women's attempts to protect themselves. I've learned to admire and appreciate women's defense systems, especially their sexual defense systems. It's not my place, or the place of any therapist, to suggest that a woman tear down the wall she may have spent years erecting. A woman may have good reasons for keeping her sexual defenses in place. I do think therapy can help women determine what those reasons are and how best to proceed: to keep the reasons and the defenses or to move beyond them.

When You Begin To Outgrow Armor

It may be that, like Joyce, the first step in outgrowing defensive armor may feel more like a breakdown than a breakthrough. The flood of feelings and memories can feel as painful as the original trauma.

Often, what brings a woman into therapy for sexual problems is that she's beginning to outgrow her armor. That is, her life situation is no longer threatening but she's still stuck inside her rigid plates of steel which are outdated, too small, awkward, isolating. As her personality and hopes and desires for her life expand, the armor begins to feel tighter and tighter.

It can actually hurt. Armor that's too tight can cause excruciating pain of its own, in body, mind, emotions and spirit. This pain can be quite independent of the original trauma. Ultimately, defensive armor can become so constrictive that it helps trigger crippling aches and pains and even life-threatening diseases, like cancer.

Barbara 2: Facing The Pain

Barbara began therapy saying she felt like a sexual freak. Her sobriety had so far meant swearing off sex — the dangerous, anonymous, mind-blowing "sick" kind that had been her special suit of armor.

When Barbara got sober she no longer felt emotionally sick and driven to unhealthy sexual encounters. But then she got physically sick, developing arthritis that was so painful she couldn't walk.

> I had the kind no doctor knew how to treat. I ached all over. And I felt constantly as if I were in danger of being squeezed to death, even when I was asleep. It took me two years to come to grips with the fact that what arthritis really meant for me was swelling in response to stress. That meant I couldn't get rid of the swelling until I got rid of the stresses.

As Barbara peeled away layer after layer of her armor to get down to the original stresses, she was able to understand that physical pain was a metaphor for emotional pain:

I had been hanging onto all this rage forever. When I began to feel better inside, I began to feel better outside. It was as if there was no difference between being swollen and achy and being sad and angry. They were all just different expressions of everything that had happened in the past. Well, there was this one big difference. I knew how to deny that I had the feelings, but I couldn't deny the physical pain. At least I couldn't deny it once I couldn't walk anymore. I had to deal with it.

For Barbara, as for many women, facing the pain was the first important step in letting go of her emotional armor against pain — and against pleasure. Let's look at some patterns of sexual response created by chronic emotional armoring rather than review individual case after case. These patterns stem from post-traumatic stress, skewed psychosexual development and sex-negative, woman-negative cultural messages — the three roots of sexual co-dependency. They represent negative ways women can express their sexual co-dependency.

Negative Styles Of Sexual Co-dependency

Women develop their styles of sexual relationship in response to needs that affect their whole lives. Here are five of the most common needs. There's nothing outlandish about them. Everyone has at least some of them. And it's usually one or more of these needs that moves women to seek out sexual relationships.

1. The need for economic security.
2. The need for positive self-image.
3. The need for nurturance.
4. The need for personal power and control.
5. The need for pleasure and satisfaction.

It's important to understand at the outset that *it is not your needs that impair sexual functioning. It is the manipulative role-playing you engage in, in the mistaken belief that your manipulations will help get these needs met.*

In my clinical practice I've found that women may develop one or more distinctly negative styles of sexual co-dependency in an attempt to get their needs met. When women develop these negative sexual styles they tend not to like themselves. These are names women have used to describe themselves when their sexual co-dependency has taken active forms: **Forever Amber, Total Woman, Ms. Goodbar, Big Bertha, Mata Hari.**

Women have used equally self-negative names when their sexual co-dependency styles have been passive: **Shrinking Violet, Sleeping Beauty, Poor Little Match Girl, Hostage Keeper, Sponge.**

Sexual styles like these not only contribute to sexual dysfunction but they can contribute to a whole negative personality profile — the kind that can lose you your job or cause an unknowing therapist to misdiagnose you as having some kind of personality disorder, even a borderline personality. Moreover, such a profile can make your recovery an uphill battle, maybe even plummet you back into the temporary relief of addictive behaviors.

Table 2.1 outlines women's needs and their self-described co-dependent sexual styles or roles. These styles develop from the roots of sexual co-dependency and they contribute to sexual dysfunction as well as to dysfunction in other aspects of relationships. They are broadly drawn to make the picture easy to see. Feel free to make additions or subtractions of your own.

A glance at Table 2.1 is enough to show that if any of these is your sexual style, you're headed for a rocky relationship. And it's double jeopardy if your partner is sexually co-dependent, too. In the words of the late Bette Davis: "Fasten your seat belts, it's going to be a bumpy night."

Moreover, you (and your partner) may not walk a smooth and easy path in therapy. You may feel utterly committed to your therapy and engaged in it, and yet you may find yourself backsliding, equivocating and above all, resisting your own feelings. Further, you may project feelings onto your therapist and attempt to create either a too-warm alliance or an antagonistic relationship. I've found that many sexual co-depen-

Table 2.1. Sexual Co-dependency: Women's Needs And Styles

Need	Active Sexual Style	Passive Sexual Style
ECONOMIC SECURITY	FOREVER AMBER grasper climber hooked on excitement SCARED	SHRINKING VIOLET victim trapped SCARED
POSITIVE SELF-IMAGE	TOTAL WOMAN projective other-defined people-pleaser SAD	SLEEPING BEAUTY introjective depressed immobilized SAD
NURTURANCE	MS. GOODBAR indispensable enabler people-pleaser fused SCARED	POOR LITTLE MATCH GIRL unable to care for self relationship addict needy ill SCARED
POWER AND CONTROL	BIG BERTHA rigid judgmental blaming ANGRY	HOSTAGE KEEPER self-blaming immobilizes partner ANGRY
PLEASURE AND SATISFACTION	MATA HARI undercover agent tease hit-and-run artist HUNGRY	SPONGE lies in wait for crumbs of pleasure sucks a partner dry HUNGRY
OTHER		

dents are skilled people-pleasers who will alter symptoms to make a therapist happy, regardless of what may be most appropriate to relieve the sexual dysfunction (rather like a partner who fakes pleasure and orgasm instead of asking for what will delight, arouse and satisfy).

Alternatively, you may be a more overt saboteur, antagonistic to both therapy and to yourself.

Characteristics Of Sexual Co-dependency

Need For Economic Security

Forever Amber: Driven by a need for economic security, she plays a culturally approved sexual role. She's active, fast and loose. A social climber, a grasper out of necessity, she sleeps with whoever can help her keep her bread buttered or literally keep food on the table. She starts out with high-powered partners but may move down the scale to involve herself with anyone, for, as she disconnects more and more from her feelings, she is likely to become hooked on the excitement of sexual conquest as well as the need for advancement. She is a prime candidate for sexual addiction. You have to look very deep inside her to see her soft center and the fear that is at her core.

Her passive counterpart is **Shrinking Violet.** Like **Amber,** she is culturally approved. She is a perennial victim, motivated by the fear (or knowledge) that she cannot support herself. She's a giving person but she wears a KICK ME sign around her neck. You'll find her staying on loyally and enduringly in relationships with losers, batterers and even HIV-infected partners she doesn't love, because she is trapped by economic need. She needs sex for reassurance, but she derives little lasting pleasure from it. **Violet** is often too terrified or ashamed to talk about her situation or seek help.

Need For A Positive Self-Image

Total Woman is moved to seek sex by a need for a positive self-image, but she projects her need onto others instead of asking it for herself. She makes her partners look good and then basks in their reflected light. She is a people-pleaser, an enabler of negative behavior in others. She slips into satin pumps and a fur-edged teddy to greet her partner with a martini — especially if her partner's an alcoholic. She may wear a smile on her face but underneath that smile is exhaustion and sadness.

Her passive counterpart is **Sleeping Beauty**, whose defenses remove her from life and immobilize her. Unable to recognize her own self, she lies in a glass case waiting to be discovered by Prince (or Princess) Charming. The glass case may consist of depression, tiredness, spaciness, agoraphobia, even heavy makeup. They all effectively keep her somewhat disengaged from her world, so that she seems not quite real. Even after discovery by Prince Charming she may retain her symptoms, because she is still disconnected from herself. Her primary emotion is sadness. She may be more enlivened by a good cry than by an orgasm.

Need For Nurturing

Ms. Goodbar is motivated by a need to nurture. This masks her own desperate need for nurturance, which she steadfastly denies. She is not so much a care-*giver* as a care-*taker*, who will kill a partner with kindness. She lacks boundaries and wants to fuse because she's afraid she doesn't really exist herself. She feels best when she's moved herself into a partner's body and soul — or walked into their eyes and shut the lids behind her, like Sheilah Graham.

Her passive counterpart is **Poor Little Match Girl**, who was deprived so much as a child that as an adult she is still a waif, one of the emotional homeless. She is especially ripe to become addicted to relationships, for she lives in the constant fear that she doesn't belong — anywhere. She'd like to belong to *you*. She is constitutionally unable to take care of her own needs and is likely to be in chronic ill health. She is an emotional black hole. No matter how much love she begs, it never seems to fill her up inside. She has sex in order to get taken care of; but her real pleasure fantasy is to be tucked into bed.

Need For Power And Control

Big Bertha is moved by the need for power and control. She's a bedroom dynamo, demanding, rigid, judgmental and blaming. Violence is a way of life for her, whether it's watching the Super Bowl, running a triathlon or yelling at the kids (who she then gathers up in bearhugs). She gets her biggest kicks in bed from expressing rage and may actually hit, bite or otherwise brutalize her partner at the moment of climax.

Her passive counterpart is **Hostage Keeper**, whose anger turns to self-blame. Pleasure is not okay for her. If she's religious, sex may even be a sin. But a sexual relationship gives her a focus for control. She keeps a partner tied up by promising and teasing without delivering.

Need For Pleasure And Satisfaction

Mata Hari, who seeks pleasure and satisfaction, is an undercover agent who very actively feeds her skin hunger while avoiding intimacy and commitment. She is a sexual hit-and-run artist, a tease who *does* deliver. Her idea of bliss is to escape for three days in a camper with an illicit lover, an endless supply of tortilla chips and no plans beyond the weekend.

Her passive counterpart is **Sponge**, who lies in wait for crumbs of pleasure. Warm and compliant, her hunger for sex is never satisfied, even when it sucks her partner dry.

These are simplifications, to be sure. But even though these roles are like cartoons, do any of them sound familiar to you? Do they *all* sound familiar? Do they sound harsh and devastating? Do they seem impossible to change? If you acknowledge that sexual roles like these can exist, where do you go from here?

Dig Deeper

In order to begin sexual recovery, it is necessary to dig deeper inside yourself to find out exactly how far you have to go and in what direction. Until you do this digging, no amount of help you might get from the outside is likely to substantially improve your life. Fritz Perls tells a story I often use in therapy situations just about at this point:

> Imagine that you are lost in the desert. You have licked the last drop of water from the rim of your canteen. You know you will die if you don't reach the oasis. If only you had a map. You pray for deliverance. Suddenly the hot wind blows a map into your hand — a map of the desert, with a big X marked "Oasis." Your prayers have been answered! Your life is saved! But as you prepare to trudge on, you realize you have no idea which direction to start in. The map is no help at all. True, there's an X marked at the oasis — but there is no X marked where YOU are. Until you find out exactly where YOU are, it doesn't matter where the oasis is. You are just as lost as you were before.

Sorry to leave you hanging like this but the story makes a point: Let's not leap into trying to find solutions for sexual co-dependency before we find out exactly what the problems are — for YOU. Having articulated the basics of the problem, let's go on to look at what actually happens in bed. How does sexual co-dependency produce toxic sex? What are the sexual specifics of the armor, the blockages and the addictive behaviors that make up sexual co-dependency? We will take an in-depth look at the anatomy of these dysfunctions next and help you find out more about where YOU are.

❧ THREE ❧

When Sex Doesn't Work: The Anatomy Of Sexual Dysfunction And Addiction

Much is known about the mechanics of sexual dysfunction. But little has been written specifically for women and next to nothing has been written about sexual co-dependency. What happens when women disconnect from their sexual selves or when their partners don't function well sexually? When sex goes awry, how does that affect women's lives? How do the sexual dysfunctions listed in the literature relate to the sexual co-dependencies outlined earlier?

These unanswered questions leave women in a one-down position around sexual recovery. Let's listen to Rebecca, the social worker you have already met who is searching for answers — and who realizes that not all the answers are inside herself.

Rebecca 2: Search For A Woman's View Of Sex

I've read the books but I can't find one that talks about *me*. I'm struggling to understand why my sexual relationship doesn't work and what can make it work. These books seem to be about somebody

else. I just don't feel that way inside. That's not the way I think about
sex, that's not the way I come to orgasm. Maybe that means I'm
totally out of line. But I think it's more likely that these books are
written by men and about men and that the world of science just
hasn't caught up with women. Or at least with me.

This chapter will try to fill the gap for Rebecca — and you
— by looking at the anatomy of sexual dysfunction and addiction from a woman's point of view. It will go beyond physiology
to discuss how sexual dysfunction affects *all* of you: body,
mind, heart and soul. And it will go beyond *you* to discuss
sexual co-dependency — how it affects your relationships.

Words Of Caution Before We Begin

First of all, sexual experience is an individual matter. Only
you can make the judgment as to whether you are sexually
functional or dysfunctional. This is not a judgment that belongs
to this book or to your doctor, your therapist or even your
partner. For instance, sexual problems may be less about sex
than about changing power balances in your relationship or in
your life. If this is true, then the answer to your problems may
be to learn to stand up for yourself out of bed as well as in bed.

Second, just because you may have a personal *Aha!* reaction
when you read a tale of sexual dysfunction, that doesn't mean
you have to rush right into therapy. You may have symptoms
but if they're not causing problems for you or your partner,
then you don't have to set out to cure them. In other words,
if it ain't broke, you don't have to fix it. Again, you are the only
person who can make that judgment.

Third, this chapter is not the *Bible* of sexual dysfunction.
Even though you may experience distressing sexual problems,
you may not find your exact symptoms listed here. Remember,
it's *your* sex life. If you think that you are dysfunctional, believe
yourself and keep searching until you find the right questions
to ask — and answers that make sense to you. You might want
to read the books in the bibliography that will tell you more
about sexual function and dysfunction.

We've all been trained to think of sex as physical, so let's start there, with what some people call the plumbing-manual approach to sexual dysfunction.

The Three Phases Of Physical Dysfunction

Current thinking says that sexual response progresses through three distinct phases: desire, excitement and orgasm. This is a valuable model to help you understand the physiology of sexual dysfunction, even though there are some built-in limitations. First, this model doesn't take into account all of the sexual dysfunctions. Second, it is a physiological model only and it doesn't take into account the relational issues or the emotional armoring we discussed in the opening chapters.

Each phase of sexual response has its own neurophysiological hookups — that is, during each phase the brain sends messages to different parts of the nervous system and elicits distinct responses. Although each phase is distinct, all three phases are interconnected as part of an overall response pattern. Let's go through the mechanics one phase at a time.

Desire

Your feelings of sexual desire or libido are triggered by your limbic system, the emotional control center of your brain, the part that activates what Freud called the id and what others call pure animal lust. Impulses are sent to your hypothalamus, which in turn triggers the secretion of endorphins and other neurotransmitters. These induce the "altered state" you associate with sexual desire: overall relaxation and well-being; acute sexual awareness; the sense of being plugged into pleasant memories and unplugged from nagging day-to-day details.

Excitement

The most dramatic physical sign of sexual arousal is dilation of the blood vessels in your genitals. This produces vaginal wetness and swelling and blushing of your clitoris and vaginal area (in a man it produces erections). Vasodilation is a reflex activity beyond your conscious control. It is triggered by centers in your spinal cord and is governed primarily by your parasympathetic nervous system. You cannot will genital engorgement and lubrication any more than a man can will an erection.

Orgasm

Orgasm is signaled by rhythmic contractions of the genital muscles. Connected with the pleasure center of your brain, orgasms most often feel indescribably good (not at all like a twitching eyelid, for example). Like excitement, orgasm is a reflex response, triggered by neural centers in your spinal column. Unlike excitement, though, it is also connected to conscious perception areas of your brain. This means that your orgasms are, to some extent, under your voluntary control. It is possible to play around with how many orgasms you can have, how long they last and how intense they are.

What Happens In Sexual Dysfunction?

Usually only one of the three phases is disrupted, at least at first. But sexual dysfunction is not always neat and tidy; one phase can disrupt another. For instance, disruption of the desire phase may mean orgasm is something you can take or leave. Or vice versa: The inability to come to orgasm may dampen your interest in seeking sex — that is, your sexual desire.

Given a big enough trauma, it is possible to blow all three phases of your sexual response system at once. If that happens, you become virtually unable to experience sexual pleasure or to respond physically to sexual stimulation.

Table 3.1 shows the primary mechanisms of the physical sexual response phases and which dysfunctions belong to which phases. It also shows analogies between men's and women's dysfunctions so that women can better understand the sexual responses of their male partners and consequently better understand their own reactions to these responses.

The most common of all the dysfunctions is low sexual desire. This affects both women and men and so I call it the Unisex Dysfunction.

Table 3.1. Physical Sexual Response Phases And Men's And Women's Dysfunctions

Response Phase	Primary Neurophysiological Mechanism	Symptom of Sexual Dysfunction	
		Women's	Men's
Desire	Limbic system and other sexual centers in brain — send pleasure messages to central nervous system.	Low desire	Low desire
Excitement	Parasympathetic nervous system in spinal column — sends message for vasodilation direct to genitals (not under your control).	Lack of lubrication	Impotence
Orgasm	Sympathetic nervous system in spinal column — sends message direct to genitals (partly under your control).	Anorgasmia	Premature ejaculation

Source: Extrapolated from *Disorders Of Sexual Desire* by Helen Singer Kaplan.

Let's outline some of the sexual dysfunctions and look at them from a clinical point of view, from a woman's point of view, and also from the perspective of co-dependent attitudes and behavior.

The Unisex Dysfunction

Low Sexual Desire

Also called **inhibited sexual desire,** *it means avoidance of sex, and it usually results in a low frequency of sexual activity. Low sexual desire is most often secondary and situational, that is, it is not inborn, but is a response to pain, to the exhaustion and overstimulation of childbirth, to relationship problems or to a traumatic event.*

It's the not-tonight-dear-I've-got-a-headache syndrome. Low sexual desire can be a major issue for you, whether it's your desire that's low or your partner's.

The definition of just how low constitutes *low* is necessarily relative, for if both of you would just as soon never have sex, then what's the problem? The difficulty arises when your desire levels don't match. This produces a hot-and-cold sexual dynamic, where one member of a couple is all set for a sizzling encounter and the other would rather tune into the 11 o'clock news.

Are You "Frigid?"

Women who avoid sex have been given an over-the-counter label through the generations, frigid. What does "frigid" really mean and how do you know if it describes you? It is a term invented by the medical system, and it is an accurate description — if you are a woman who's literally frozen and immobilized at the prospect of sex.

"Frigid" has a locker-room connotation, too, a put-down, patronizing tone. It pathologizes women who won't "put out" and illegitimizes their real reasons for not wanting sex.

Are you "frigid?" It does not mean your desire is pathologically low if you turn away unwanted advances, if you've been working 12 hours a day and would rather sleep than make love, or if your partner wants you to dress up in a black leather garter belt every night like a dominatrix and you find yourself fantasizing about a month alone in Alaska with a pile of murder mysteries. Rather, it may mean you need to work out with your would-be partner what would be *mutually* satisfying in terms of sex.

What Is Low Sexual Desire?

Women have by no means cornered the market on low sexual desire. Contrary to the great American myth that all men are ready for sex at the drop of a lace handkerchief, men can have low sexual desire, too.

But whether your partner is a man or a woman, if he or she wants sex more than you do, you can feel put upon and objectified, as if your body is all you're any good for. On the other hand, if you are hot for more sex in your life, a partner's low desire can seem like the Chinese water torture. As one woman complains:

It's the constant hurt and rejection that finally got to me and made me crazy. I've stopped bringing it up any more because I know he'll be too busy, or too tired, or too disapproving or too something or other. The plain matter of it is, he just doesn't want to make love with me.

How Does It Develop?

Why do women develop low sexual desire? For starters, women enter sexual relationships for the variety of reasons mentioned: security, nurturing, enhanced self-image, power, pleasure.

When their constellation of expectations is not met, their enthusiasm for sex can plummet to the sub-basement. In addition, the roots of women's low sexual desire can be post-traumatic. If women are holding onto the fear, anger and hurt that belong to old scenes in their lives, then it's virtually impossible for them to feel and express present erotic feelings at the same time — unless they successfully split off from the old feelings. (This is a mechanism we'll look at later, when we discuss sexual addiction.)

Men develop low desire for the same reasons: post-traumatic stress and/or unmet present expectations.

Low Sexual Desire And Sexual Co-dependency

Low sexual desire can certainly be a result of co-dependency in the relationship. It can arise from any of the three roots of co-dependency: the post-traumatic stress mentioned above, also skewed psychosexual development and the cultural double message that women are supposed to enjoy pleasing men but aren't supposed to enjoy sex. (The cultural counterpart for men is the male performance trip that says men are supposed to be Super Studs.) Passive roles like **Sleeping Beauty** and **Shrinking Violet** are prone to low sexual desire.

Also, a partner's low sexual desire can trigger co-dependent responses from women who depend wholly upon their partner for their sexual identity and pleasure. Pushy **Big Bertha**, ever-pleasing **Total Woman**, and ever-needy **Little Match Girl** are roles that can easily emerge when your partner is turned off sex.

Women's Sexual Dysfunctions

Inability To Come To Orgasm

Also called anorgasmia or orgasmic dysfunction, this means it's impossible for you to experience the delightful physical discharge of sexual tension known as orgasm. Primary anorgasmia means you've never been able to experience orgasm. The more hopeful term is preorgasmic — you haven't been able to experience orgasm yet. Secondary anorgasmia means a relatively recent and perhaps temporary difficulty, perhaps caused by a specific situation like a trauma, a fight with your partner or not enough stimulation to excite you to climax.

Being unable to come to orgasm can sometimes be devastating for women. For starters, it can be extremely frustrating, especially if you are continually turned on during sex and continually let down, just as you're about to bubble up over the edge. If you were a man, you might describe the feeling as "blue balls." Women describe the feeling as "hung up," "high and dry," "climbing the walls." Some women know the feeling mainly by its emotional aftereffects, such as "waking up the next morning feeling like a bitch."

Because there's so much focus in our culture on orgasm as a sexual goal, being unable to come to orgasm can throw your whole concept of normality into question — especially if you're an Adult Daughter who isn't too clear what normal means anyway, let alone what sexually normal means.

This is most poignantly true if you've never come to orgasm in your whole life. You may wonder why on earth people bother to spend so much time thinking about sex or having it. You may desperately wish you could have orgasms — and multiorgasms, "just like everybody else." But since you don't know firsthand what an orgasm is, you don't know how to go about getting one for yourself and you secretly wonder if you would recognize one if it leapt up and bit you on the nose.

This question of recognition reminds me of a touching story told to me years ago by my friend Anni, whose toddler years were spent in a Nazi concentration camp:

> We were starving and my older sister would try to comfort me by reciting to me endless descriptions of food. The problem was, I was too young to know half of what she was talking about. I would become crazed whenever she told me about pineapple cake — because I couldn't remember having ever tasted pineapple cake. She'd talk about the beautiful glossy layers and the tantalizing tastes and I couldn't even make a picture of them in my head. I used to scream at her that pineapple cake didn't exist.

The message of this story is this: The orgasms you've never experienced are like Anni's pineapple cake. First of all, they do exist, even if you've never had one. Second, they are a possibility for every woman — but you may have to get out of concentration camp before you can find out what they are or maybe even imagine them.

That is, in order to experience orgasm you may have to free yourself, body, mind, heart and soul.

Reasons For Anorgasmia

If you want to come to orgasm and it isn't happening for you, there may be a number of reasons why and these reasons may be complex. Maybe the answer is simply that you're not getting enough of the right kind of stimulation. On the other hand, the answer may be deeper. The clinical image I often get is that a woman is heavily armored and *holding on tight* — most often to anger or rage. Perhaps she is angry at a present

partner, perhaps at the murky past. Perhaps she is holding on
to a scene that is so terrifying that the letting go into orgasm
will reduce all her carefully constructed defenses to rubble.
Such scenes often involve incest, rape and abandonment.

Orgasm dysfunctions can cause relationship problems. This
can be true whether your partner is a man or a woman. The
confusion and frustration can cause explosions — both in bed
and out. Orgasm dysfunctions can also be the *result* of relationship problems. If you perceive your partner as being insensitive, inept, self-absorbed (you know, the cartoon of the
callous lout who rolls over and goes to sleep as soon as he's
got what he wants), your orgasms will suffer and so will your
relationship. Conversely, a partner with performance anxiety
who is constantly plucking at you and asking "Didja come?"
can be just as much of a turnoff.

Orgasmic Function And Sexual Co-dependency

Sexual co-dependency can exacerbate problems of orgasm
for women. If any of the following comes close to describing
you, you might want to examine your own co-dependencies:

1. You feel you should help your partner come to orgasm.
   There's nothing wrong with wanting to be an expert
   lover, but if the "shoulds" weigh heavily on you or if you
   find yourself downplaying your own satisfaction, then
   you're in trouble. **Total Woman** is a role you can play to
   the hilt. You may even have the little vamp outfit to wear
   on special occasions.
2. You grew up believing sexual pleasure was bad, or you
   had no education about how to give yourself sexual
   pleasure or heighten the sexual pleasure you can get
   from your partner. You are essentially a bystander in the
   sexual scene. You expect your partner to give you an
   orgasm and you desperately wish he or she would come
   through for you. Co-dependent roles that are familiar to
   you are passive ones, like **Sleeping Beauty** and **Sponge**.

If you get frustrated enough to blame your partner for not coming through, **Big Bertha** might emerge.

3. You are a victim of the cultural conditioning that says all sex is goal-oriented sex. This includes the "big bang" theory of sexual satisfaction: Orgasm is the only goal. If you're not having orgasms on demand, you think there must be something desperately wrong with you. Or wrong with your partner. To compensate, you are likely to role-play. **Big Bertha** might be your choice: a woman with high sexual desire, but with little satisfaction to show for it — and a load of rage. Or you might retreat into **Shrinking Violet** or **Sleeping Beauty.**

Vaginismus

This is chronic, involuntary spasm of the vaginal entrance, which makes intercourse painful or impossible. Vaginismus is a post-traumatic response. Traumas that cause vaginismus include incest and rape. Medical traumas can also trigger vaginismus. These include episiotomy, the cutting of your vaginal opening to facilitate childbirth, and so-called "love surgery," taking a tuck in your vagina to tighten it for your male partner's pleasure.

Although vaginismus does not fit neatly into the three-phase model, it is nonetheless recognized as a distinct if somewhat rare, sexual dysfunction. It is one of the most graphic ways a woman's body can play out its memories of physical, emotional or spiritual abuse. The vagina simply shuts the door. Do Not Enter. No penis allowed, and in extreme cases, no finger or no gynecologist's speculum, either.

Vaginismus does not always pose a sexual problem for a woman. For instance, vaginal penetration may not be how she wants to make love, especially if she's in a lesbian relationship. And vaginismus tends not to affect a woman's capacity for desire or for orgasm — the hookups are separate, so to speak. So, although it's consistently named in the medical literature as a sexual dysfunction, it's appropriate to ask: Is it a sexual *dys*function, or is it a defense that has made it possible for a woman to continue to *function* sexually through post-traumatic stress? Vaginismus may cause fewer problems for a woman than for a male partner who wants intercourse.

Vaginismus And Sexual Co-dependency

How does vaginismus impact on sexual co-dependency? In at least three ways, all of them in relation to men:

1. If you are a **Total Woman** or a **Ms. Goodbar** who gets your major satisfaction by pleasing a male partner, you will probably feel you're letting him down because you're not able to have intercourse.
2. If you are a **Shrinking Violet** who needs to rely on his approval rather than work things out equally, then sex will probably be a disaster — because you probably won't get his approval.
3. Whatever role you play, if your only vision of normal is to be able to have "real" sex (i.e., intercourse), then you will feel abnormal no matter how sexually responsive you are or how orgasmic.

Genital Pain

*Also called **dyspareunia**, this means pain on genital stimulation, especially vaginal pain on intercourse. Its causes are vaginal infection, lack of lubrication, injury, surgical trauma, remembered trauma and sexual violence.*

Genital pain can affect all phases of women's sexual response: desire, excitement and orgasm. If your vagina is red, raw and hurting, or if you have bacterial or interstitial cystitis, the last thing on your mind is likely to be sex, especially intercourse.

One of the causes of genital pain is infection, which can also infect your partner and which you may have caught from your partner in the first place. The possibilities for guilt, rage, blame and self-blame become endless here. And the problems are compounded when you can't talk about what's going on or when you have a sexual partner who's insensitive to your well-being.

Infections that can raise havoc with your genitals and your sex life include some of the sexually transmitted diseases (or STDs). One of these is herpes, an incurable virus that causes lesions on your cervix, vagina or vulva, and also systemic flu-like symptoms and tingling pain. Another infection is *monilia,* otherwise known as yeast, *candidiasis* or *candida albicans.* This produces a discharge similar to cottage cheese and an itch that will drive you to distraction. I once had a client who had been diagnosed with a personality disorder. She turned out to have a chronic untreated yeast infection, which she was afraid to tell anyone about. It was literally making her act crazy — and think she was going crazy.

Lack of vaginal lubrication can cause pain on intercourse. Vaginal lubrication lessens during and after menopause as part of the normal aging process. Alternatively, lack of vaginal lubrication may point to a problem in the excitement phase of your sexual encounters. There can be a number of causes, ranging from fear of sex to not enough of the right kind of stimulation.

Injury, including surgical trauma, can leave temporary or permanent genital pain. A common injury is episiotomy during childbirth, which may hurt only for a matter of weeks, or it might leave a permanent and painful scar at your vaginal opening. Forced intercourse and memories of forced intercourse can also cause pain — and pain that lasts.

Genital pain is second cousin to vaginismus, and may be a warning signal that vaginismus will follow. Or it may be the first sign that the condition of vaginismus exists.

Genital Pain And Sexual Co-dependency

These can interact in the following ways:

1. **Sleeping Beauty** may not be aware of pain or infection until it becomes out of control.
2. **Poor Little Match Girl** and **Shrinking Violet** lack financial and emotional recourses to care for themselves. They

will allow a minor infection to become a roaring one that makes their lives miserable for a long time. They will also be overwhelmed with guilt for having contracted a vaginal infection.

Alternatively, they will put up with endless amounts of pain in order to keep their partners happy.
3. **Big Bertha** will blame the pain or disease on her partner, whether her partner deserves it or not.
4. **Hostage Keeper** will blame herself for hurting — until it hurts her partner, too.

Men's Sexual Dysfunctions

"Premature" Ejaculation

This is lack of control over ejaculatory reflex; most often experienced as "men who come too soon." It is caused by genital anesthesia, which makes a man unaware of exactly when he is about to come to orgasm and therefore unable to pace himself. This is analogous to women's orgasmic problems, as it is part of the same mechanism.

The way our culture treats boys while they are growing up might as well be a training program for premature ejaculation. Taboos against masturbation and lack of instruction about sexual pleasure teach them to "relieve" themselves in the bathroom behind closed doors — and to do it quickly before they get caught by whoever comes knocking at the door to find out why they're in there so long.

Premature ejaculation is the most common sexual dysfunction for men. Its very label puts men down (have you ever heard of *mature* ejaculation?). Besides, sexologists can't agree on a precise definition of what "too soon" means. Masters and Johnson say it's when a man reaches orgasm before his partner does *50% of the time.*

But think about your own life for a moment. If you're a woman who enjoys intercourse, how long do you need to have intercourse last in order for you to experience orgasm or other satisfaction? A minute? An hour? Does the time vary? Are there any other variables besides time — like the closeness you feel during intercourse or the energy flow between you and your partner? Are you satisfied by sexual behaviors other than intercourse? From the interviews I've had with various women it seems obvious that satisfaction varies tremendously from woman to woman and from situation to situation.

Despite the difficulties in reaching an absolute definition of what it is, coming too soon is a male sexual problem that directly affects women who depend on intercourse for sexual satisfaction. A "premature" partner can be the height of frustration. You feel aroused without release; tortured and tantalized. When you are frustrated enough, you may develop problems coming to orgasm or you may stop wanting to have sex at all.

Premature Ejaculation And Sexual Co-dependency

This dysfunction wreaks havoc most when it combines with sexual co-dependency to produce a volatile relationship reaction.

1. Partners don't talk openly about what's going on. One scenario is that He feels bad about his performance and She (in the guise of **Total Woman**) leaps to rescue his wounded ego instead of going for what she wants.
2. Women sulk and don't ask for what they want, playing passive roles like **Sponge** and **Sleeping Beauty.**
3. Women make assumptions about what coming too soon means: *He does it just to taunt me. It feels like a form of sexual abuse.* They base their actions on this guesswork and become **Poor Little Match Girl** — the neediest woman on the block.
4. Men who can't control their ejaculations avoid closeness to avoid the embarrassment of coming too soon, causing women to feel uncontacted, uncared for and unloved. At this point, premature ejaculation may become a control issue, inspiring women to play their co-dependent roles

— actively as **Big Bertha** and passively as **Hostage Keeper.** The stated or unstated message goes like this:
You are a failure and I'm never going to let you forget it. We may never talk about this directly but for the rest of our lives, you OWE me. So it's a trade-off for me. The sex is terrible but as long as we keep things the way they are, I'll have an emotional edge over you.

"Impotence"

This is the inability to get or maintain an erection. The origins may be physiological: injury, substance abuse, smoking, diabetes, high blood pressure medication. Origins may also be psychological or borne in the relationship, such as co-dependency with its attendant stress, depression and performance anxiety. **Primary impotence** *means never having experienced an erection.* **Secondary impotence** *means impotence that develops later in life.*

There's a semantic problem in a diagnosis of impotence. The current theory is that the word "impotence" is demeaning. That is, it puts a man down by defining his whole self by how his penis lets him down. The more upbeat names for this dysfunction are now "erectile dysfunction" and "erectile incompetence." In my clinical experience, however, these terms are not all that uplifting and impotence may actually be the more useful word — because what we really are talking about is lack of power or loss of power.

Let me explain. Most of the men who have come into my office with erectile problems have developed them because, indeed, they do lack power in some significant aspect of their lives. This is true whether the loss of erectile control is a response to present problems, such as partner or job, or past problems, such as growing up in an abusive family. Any situation that produces fear, anger, tension or exhaustion can contribute. Co-dependency may well cause lack of power, especially when co-dependency is the result of post-traumatic stress. Even when erectile problems have a purely physiological cause, such as alcohol use, diabetes or low testosterone levels, there is a power imbalance at some level which must be addressed.

Whatever the loss of power, a parasympathetic reaction is triggered over which men have no control (see Table 3.1). The signal is short-circuited; blood vessels do not dilate. The penis lies limp and flaccid no matter how much stimulation it gets and no matter how much its owner desperately wills himself to have an erection.

I have found that it is precisely this double whammy — loss of power and loss of control — that causes erectile difficulties. So this is the spirit in which I use the word "impotence." It may not be a perfect word but at least it calls a spade a spade and gives us an image to work with.

It doesn't take a big leap of imagination to guess how impotence affects women who depend on intercourse for their sexual satisfaction. To add insult to injury, women who are socialized to believe that intercourse is the only normal way to have sex are left optionless and unsatisfied. They may become depressed or violently angry. Their self-esteem may plummet, as may their esteem for their partner. They may turn to outside relationships (which poses a real physical danger in this age of AIDS) and they may finally leave the relationship to find a "real" man.

Impotence And Sexual Co-dependency

It is not difficult to imagine how impotence affects sexual co-dependency and vice versa.

1. Men are supposed to be powerful. After all, most messages in our culture say so. Impotence is a disproof of the great American myth that men go through life with on-demand erections that allow them to stay perpetually on top, in the missionary position.
2. There are also issues of pleasure, of giving and receiving. If a woman is a compulsive giver, how come she isn't a good enough lover to give her man an erection? If she plays such a good game of **Total Woman**, how come he isn't playing **Total Man**?

3. If a woman depends on a man's erect penis in order to feel sexually normal — well, when the penis goes down, the jig is up.

Emotional And Spiritual Dysfunctions

While it is helpful to understand the sexual dysfunctions that sexologists recognize, it's also crucial to understand that this is not the whole story of why sex doesn't work for women. Women often come into my office with sexual dysfunctions not mentioned in the literature.

The co-dependency connections implicit even in the physical dysfunctions show that making love passionately and sanely involves much more than genitals and orgasm. It involves even more than the whole body. It involves the total personality, including intellect, emotions and spirituality. Further, whole-person lovemaking doesn't happen in a vacuum. It happens in context — the context of your life, your relationships, your memory, your total *self,* and how your total self approaches sexual pleasure.

In looking at why sex doesn't work, I think it's important that we add two more dysfunctions to the list:

• Inhibited initiation
• Whole-person disconnection.

Inhibited Initiation

This dysfunction looks like low sexual desire but it is a communication disorder, not a desire disorder. Women with inhibited initiation want sex but they don't know how to ask for it or even how to put themselves in situations where sex might be a possibility.

This is the Don't Ask dysfunction. It affects countless women no matter what their age, class, race, sexual orientation, or partner status — single or partnered. Although you won't find it in the sexological literature, it's a dysfunction that very much belongs in a woman's guide to sexual recovery.

Inhibited initiation begins in the mists of our sex-negative, woman-negative cultural conditioning. Throughout history, women (at least Good and Modest women) have been socialized not to ask for what they want and certainly not to make the first moves. Although this dynamic is changing with the times, it will doubtless continue for most women unless there is a wholesale cultural revolution.

This social prohibition has three direct consequences:

1. It maintains a low sexual profile for women, thereby protecting them, to some extent, from dangerous sexual encounters.
2. It leaves sexual impetus in the hands of men.
3. It becomes a learned disability for many women and a specific sexual dysfunction.

Remember back to your own girlhood. If you're like most of us, it was the boy who was supposed to ask you for a date, offer the first goodnight kiss, lure you into the back seat of the bus or his family car. Bumbling though his approaches may have been, he at least got a great deal of practice you never got. (Imagine trying to play The Emperor Concerto without having done your five-finger exercises first. You'd probably give up before you ever reached the piano.)

If you never got to practice, you may have problems now initiating sexual encounters. This not only cuts down your possibilities for a date on Saturday night (in the words of Woody Allen) but it also leaves you dangerously vulnerable in this age of AIDS and date rape. If the control is always with your partner, you are a potential victim, especially if you're a **Forever Amber** or **Shrinking Violet** who can't say No.

Even in established and safe relationships, being unable to initiate amounts to not being able to ask for what you want. This can loom as a particularly distressing problem for lesbian couples because both are socialized the same way — as women. Once the flush of hot new lust is over, lovemaking can grind to a halt if neither woman has the practice or confidence to continue initiating sex. Humorist Kate Clinton refers to this as Lesbian Bed Death. Viewed from the co-dependency construct in Table 2.1, it's like two **Sleeping Beauties**, lying side by side in separate glass cases.

In this dysfunction of sexual communication there is much room for the co-dependency connections. They are there in the passive victim roles like **Sleeping Beauty, Sponge** and **Shrinking Violet**, who depend on their partners to make the moves, and in the **Total Woman,** who is so expert at nurturing others but who would rather eat lizards than divulge what *she* wants.

Whole-Person Disconnection

This is disempowering sex; the opposite of sexual ecstasy. A constellation of sexual processes that are unsensual, dispirited and unsatisfying. Whether or not it is accompanied by physical dysfunction, whole-person disconnection usually means a relationship is experienced as rigid, proscribed, closed and senseless. It constricts rather than expands a relationship with a partner.

This is among the most challenging of the sexual dysfunctions. It is also the most difficult to describe precisely because its symptoms are more than physical. There is no way of accurately measuring the emotional and spiritual disturbances central to whole-person sexual disconnection. They are evident in all the active and passive co-dependency roles from **Forever Amber** through **Hostage Keeper.**

You are experiencing whole-person disconnection when you feel any of the following in conjunction with sex:

- Boredom instead of playfulness and romance
- Hatred or pity instead of love
- Escape fantasies instead of commitment
- Hurtfulness instead of nurturing
- Withholding instead of intimacy
- Fear instead of joy.

Rather than fill paragraphs with abstract words, I am going to let women speak — and ask that you use your imagination to see if their descriptions fit you.

Julia 2: Rage

We have already met Julia. Her whole-person disconnection began with the trauma of growing up in an alcoholic, incestuous family and was intensified by post-partum intercourse forced on her by her husband. She is no longer able to come to orgasm—or able to feel sexual at all. A total **Total Woman**, she feels guilt at being sexually numb and tries to make up for it by overnurturing Carl, behavior which she is coming increasingly to resent. For Julia, nurturing has become a sexual and spiritual dysfunction.

> I'm so angry sometimes I just want to pound on him. But what do I do? I grit my teeth and do something more to try to please him. He went away on business, and I wallpapered the whole dining room. I thought he'd love me for it. But he just sort of grunted. I think he didn't really like the pattern. Sometimes I think my rage is a substitute for the sexual feelings I used to have.

Lou And Maddy: Fusion

This is another example of whole-person disconnection. The context is different from Julia and Carl because the couple seems so close rather than so distant. In fact, the couple is fused and Lou has problems maintaining a sense of herself when she is with Maddy. How they make love reflects this loss of self.

Lou has been with Maddy for seven years. They not only live together, they also run a public relations business together and have many friends in common. Lou describes Maddy as rigid, controlling and possessive, and also as beautiful, charismatic and exciting.

> I feel confused around her a lot. As though she were somehow co-opting my personality, using it for her own purposes. And yet Maddy turns me on. She's bright, imaginative and full of fun.
>
> When we make love, we have to do it her way — always. More and more, I've been feeling totally *blah* after lovemaking instead of relaxed and expressive the way I used to feel. She comes to orgasm

and I just feel *So What?* I come to orgasm and I feel I could do it better by myself with my vibrator.

I want her to love me passionately, irresponsibly. I want her to strew me with roses. We make love but it's just sort of going through the motions and I have the feeling I could be anybody. Her eyes look at me but I don't think they ever see me. When I wake up the next morning, I feel deflated like a balloon that's lost its air overnight.

Where is the arc of energy that used to flow between us that would connect our hearts and our minds? That's what sex is all about for me and that's what's missing now. I think it's because I no longer trust Maddy as a person. I see her as so involved with herself that what I want is not really important to her. We get turned on but we're only sex objects for each other. To me she's exciting and vibrant and to her I've been a willing slave. There's no blending of our spirits any more when we make love. Unless I want to lose myself entirely I have to pull back and not be involved with her.

When You Want Too Much: Sexual Obsession And Addiction

Sexual dysfunction doesn't always mean turning off sex. For some women, it means turning *on* to sex — alcoholically and co-dependently. This is not to say that all women who look forward to sex and enjoy it are sexual addicts or that you're sexually obsessive if you happen to fall in love and can't think of anything except when you're next going to get to go to bed with your lover. Sex is supposed to be exciting and fun, and there may be times when it's appropriate for it to be right up there at the top of your list. But for some women, sex *is* out of control, and it has become a persistently negative part of their lives.

Women who want too much sex — or who want sex too much — have been called various names in our culture, none of them complimentary. They're the nymphos, whores, loose women, fast women, teases. They're the ball breakers, the castrating bitches, the unholy ones. They're the kind of girl no mother wants her son to marry.

When this happens, the concept of "too much" has been decided not by you but by somebody else. Your sexual desire is defined as a moral issue and a personality problem. This means that if you're a woman who wants too much, you may have a hard time finding support, even if you want to kick the habit.

How do you begin to find out if you're a woman who wants too much? Sex may be a problem for you if you find yourself doing any of the following:

10 Signs Of Sexual Obsession And Addiction

1. Using sex to avoid intimacy with yourself or your partner.
2. Needing sex much more than you used to and enjoying it much less.
3. Never having enough sex, even though you acknowledge you have a lot.
4. Being miserable if every sexual encounter is not perfect.
5. Replaying old sexual scenarios in unsatisfying ways.
6. Thinking about sex to the exclusion of other things that are important to you.
7. Inappropriately sexualizing your relationships — for instance with your co-workers or with your children.
8. Getting into (or staying in) unsafe relationships because of the sex.
9. Making sexual decisions that hurt yourself or make you ill.
10. Making sexual decisions that hurt your significant others, including your children.

Obsession, Addiction And Sexual Co-dependency

The process of sexual addiction, like the process of any other addiction, is a defense. A defense against feeling whatever in your life is intolerable.

To understand why women develop the defensive armor that is sexual obsession and addiction, let's go back to the roots of co-dependency — that triangle of post-traumatic stress, skewed psychosexual development and a sex-negative, woman-negative culture. When the impact of this triangle is big enough and overwhelming enough, one possible course of action is to disown your own negative experiences — to split off from them so that you don't feel them any more.

This existential split is a survival mechanism. Actually it is a brilliant one, for it allows you to function relatively happily under conditions that might otherwise land you in the mad-house or worse. It's a disappearing act; when you're under attack, you simply vanish. A medical name for this is *schizoid split;* you may sometimes feel as if you're leading two lives or maybe even more.

If this is your style of defense, then you may be able to enjoy sex a great deal — but only up to a point. Because you have effectively learned to split off from your own experience, you have no way of integrating sexual pleasure into your life, and you are ripe for developing sexual obsessions and addictions.

Popcorn-Bowl Syndrome

Popcorn-Bowl Syndrome is kind of like noshing on your favorite munchies while you watch television. You're not fully aware of what you're eating, so you reach in the bowl again and again, and you are genuinely surprised when the bowl is empty. You still have the taste in your mouth and your head — and it tastes like *more.* You root around for more goodies to satisfy your cravings.

Here's a summary of this cycle of sexual obsession and addiction:

- **Existential Split:**
  You are constitutionally unable to integrate sex into the rest of your life.
- **Unaware Reaching:**
  Since you never experience integrated satisfaction, you need more and more stimulation and perhaps increasingly ritualized forms of stimulation, which may take extraordinary amounts of time, energy and money.
- **Wanting Too Much:**
  No matter how much stimulation you have, you are never

quite satisfied, or never satisfied for very long, so that you want more sex than you can possibly integrate.

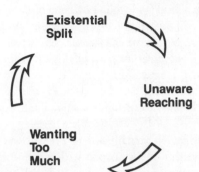

Existential Split

Unaware Reaching

Wanting Too Much

Figure 3.1. Popcorn Bowl Syndrome: The Cycle Of Sexual Obsession And Addiction.

Sexual Obsession, Sexual Addiction And Co-dependency

Both sexual obsession and addiction are basically co-dependent forms of sexual relating. You may play them out as any of the actively co-dependent roles. **Forever Amber** sleeping up the ladder of success, **Total Woman** the perennial sweetheart, so eager to please, **Ms. Goodbar** the earth mother who smothers with sensuality, **Big Bertha** who wants her sex on demand and **Mata Hari** the hit-and-run artist.

Throughout this section, we've been speaking of sexual obsession and sexual addiction in the same breath, but there is a difference. Broadly speaking, obsession means thinking about it and addiction means doing it. For instance, Barbara describes herself as an addict and Jennifer describes herself as obsessive.

Barbara 3: No Is Not Enough

You remember Barbara who used to bar-hop. She calls

herself a sexual freak — an addict who has sworn off sex altogether and is now terrified to resume.

> I grew up as a "bad" girl. You know, one of those cute kids that would take care of the whole football team after the game — it was sure better than going home and listening to my mother get beat up by my father or getting beat up myself. I got married once but that was mainly to get away from home. It was really boring and I couldn't see cheating on him, he was much too sweet. So we just drifted apart. I think about him sometimes and wonder how he's doing.
>
> I used to see myself on a mission to save the world — through love. I was a pushover for anyone with a sob story. I thought I could help everyone just by going to bed with them. I honestly did. I liked that part of myself. I still do. I was so passionate. In my heyday I could have written a best-selling book: *Women Who Come Too Much.*
>
> But my passions kept landing me on my ear. I never understood that. It's one of the great disappointments of my life. I can't understand how I could have been so full of ideals and love and been so zapped by it. Finally I got scared and quit all that running around. AIDS for one thing — you just don't know who has it. So I went cold turkey. Then I got really sick and that didn't seem fair.
>
> At this point I know I'm not going to start up all that sex again because it's too scary. But why do I get sick when I stop? It seems I'm damned if I do and damned if I don't.

Barbara's statement describes sexual co-dependency in an addictive form. Sex is not the problem for Barbara and so just saying No to sex isn't enough to make her life feel better. She needs to deal with the roots of her wanting too much.

Jennifer 1: Spiralling Thoughts

Obsessed with intercourse, Jennifer is married to Martin, who is unable to have erections. Her story demonstrates the struggle to identify sexual needs and come to terms with them.

> I grew up thinking that love meant intercourse. I never saw love expressed any other way. My father was a doctor — a GP in a

small city. All the women came to him because he was the best doctor in town. He was the handsomest, too, and I think he must have had over 20 mistresses while I was growing up. Anyway, he was hardly ever home and my mother was always in tears. She finally took to her bed and just pined away. I was an only child. I didn't know what to do. She'd close her door and I'd just leave her alone. One day she never got up. She'd taken a whole bottle of the Demerol Dad got for her to quiet her nerves.

I vowed I'd never let anything like that happen to me. So when I met Martin I made sure we had lots and lots of sex. If we went to sleep without having sex I made sure we had it in the morning before he went off to work.

We were happy for years that way — and then Martin opened up his own business at home. I think it was that very first day he didn't leave the house to go to work that the problem began. We started to make love and then a great big bundle of nothing happened. He couldn't get an erection.

After a couple of weeks of this, I began to get very upset that he didn't love me any more. And after a couple of months we went to see a sex therapist. Things really started to spiral then because everything we did just seemed to make the problem worse. Martin even had injections he could give himself to make him hard but he got a reaction to them — his erection wouldn't go down and we ended up in the emergency room. I'm sure the whole hospital was laughing at us.

In spite of this I still needed to have intercourse and he couldn't give it to me. I was beside myself. Literally. One part of me was continuing to have a relationship with my husband and the other part was beginning to have hallucinations. I began to imagine that men would come into my bed and have sex with me. Just have their way with me and then leave.

That was when I realized I was staying in bed all day with the door closed, just like my mother.

The next day I went to a Sex and Love Anonymous group. They helped me understand that I wasn't sick and crazy but that I was just responding to sick and crazy stuff that had never been talked about in my family. I wasn't morally wrong. That was really important for me to find out. But all the same, I was helping to create a pretty sick system between me and my husband.

So that's where I am now. I'm ready to stop making things worse but I still don't know how to make things better. Also I still think about intercourse all the time. I don't know how to think about sex any other way.

So far we've named sexual co-dependency, affirmed the fact of women's defensive armor and the need for it and outlined characteristics of sexual dysfunction and addiction, the reasons that sex doesn't work. Before moving on to the positive side of sexual co-dependency and the task of detoxing your sexual relationships, here is a self-assessment guide so that you can evaluate where you need to begin to work to help yourself make love in a more whole-person, satisfying way.

Sexual Co-dependency: A Self-Assessment Guide

Is your sex dysfunctional or addictive? How do these sexual patterns impact on the rest of your life? To make your own assessment, complete Table 3.2 adding any categories of your own to tailor it to your personal situation.

Table 3.2 lists sexual problems discussed in chapter 3 and relates them to co-dependency issues discussed in chapters 1 and 2. Remember, it shows only the negative aspects of your sexual relationships. We will discuss the positive aspects, along with suggestions about what to do with the negative aspects, later.

Table 3.2. Sexual Co-dependency Self-Assessment Guide

Your or Your Partner's Dysfunction	Your Need (Security Self-Image Nurturing Power/Control Pleasure)	Your Style	
		Active Co-dependent Roles (Forever Amber, Total Woman, Ms. Goodbar, Big Bertha, Mata Hari)	Passive Co-dependent Roles (Shrinking Violet, Sleeping Beauty, Match Girl, Hostage Keeper, Sponge)
Low Desire			
Anorgasmia			
Genital Pain Or Vaginismus			
Premature Ejaculation			
Impotence			
Inhibited Initiation			
Whole-Person Disconnection			
Wanting Too Much			
Other			

❈ FOUR ❈

Sexual Wholeness:
The Positive Side Of
Sexual Co-dependency

If you could write an ad for an ideal lover, what would it say? If you wanted to represent yourself as the most sexually nurturing and intimate partner you could possibly be, what qualities would you want to include? Chances are, you'd include some of the very characteristics that belong to the co-dependent sexual styles we met in the first three chapters.

This may sound like a contradiction, especially considering that we have been discussing the problems created by sexual co-dependency. But if you stop to look at the total picture, you can see that sexual co-dependency is not all problematic, not by a long shot. That's what can make it so confusing, both to the co-dependent and to a partner.

Among the negative patterns of co-dependency are a healthy number of positive, warm, energetic qualities that can actually enhance sexual recovery and pleasure. They are qualities like intuitiveness, playfulness, openness and passion that make life worth living and make sex worth having. Qualities that move women to admit:

If you want to know the truth, I *like* being co-dependent. Sometimes recovery feels like such a drag. So self-righteous and serious.

What's so bad about co-dependency? Aren't we all dependent on each other to some extent? I mean what would happen if we gave all that up and just whirled around in our own separate orbits?

Let me hasten to say that the object of sexual recovery is not total independence from your partner. Nor is it to take away everything that's close and fun in your sex life — anymore than changing to a healthier way of eating means taking away all the foods that taste good. The object of sexual recovery is to help you tone down negative dynamics and tone up positive ones. In short, the object is to put you in a strong position of choice about your sexuality. From this position you can move in a number of directions which will help enable you to do the following:

• Understand your sexual responses.
• Enhance your sexual responses.
• Choose a safe and satisfying partner.
• Choose the kind of sex you want.
• Communicate your sexual desires.

To anyone who says sexual co-dependency is all bad, I say: There's a flip side to sexual co-dependency, and that flip side is healthy and allows growth. It has to do with the give and take between partners — and also between the parts of your self. Let's call it sexual wholeness.

What Is Sexual Wholeness?

Sexual wholeness is a pleasurable pattern of lovemaking in which one's attitudes and behaviors are habitually determined by one's self — and enhanced by a partner.
It means you consistently rely on *you* to provide your sense of sexual self. You are aware of your inner center of sexual wisdom and serenity and how to tap into it. Your sexual

responses reflect that center, so that you are giving clear messages to your partner.

It means you have developed rewarding patterns of sexual behavior in all phases of your sexual relationship, including the ability to choose a partner who is willing to cooperate with you — able both to give and receive.

It means your mating dance is in control, however loud and fast the music may play. It is based on mutual trust rather than mutual manipulation.

It means give *and* take in sexual relationships, and that you organize your sexual encounters around satisfaction — yours and your partner's.

In sexual wholeness, your sexual expectations are based on your actual experience. You are able to tell if a relationship feels good to you. You are able to separate good present feelings from painful old emotional tapes. You are able to trust your present feelings and build on the trust. Conversely, you can tell when a sexual relationship doesn't feel good, and when it doesn't you are able to take measures to change the relationship or end it.

You develop bedroom roles that help you get what you want. And you do this in a way that ensures intimacy and closeness with your partner — and at the same time ensures autonomy.

You and your partner are aware of each other's sexual roles, expectations and behaviors.

You feel generally satisfied by how your sexual relationship is going, no matter whether your sexual encounters are frequent or infrequent.

You can accept your capacity for sexual cooperation even though you may have experienced it only intermittently or with only one partner.

The road from sexual co-dependency to sexual wholeness and interdependence may not be quick and easy but it is certainly possible.

A crucial step is to understand that you developed your sexual co-dependencies for basically healthy reasons, all to do with surviving your life situations. Think about the skills it took to create these roles — skills you sharpened in response to stress. And think about how maintaining these roles now takes stick-to-itiveness — that capacity for long-term endurance you developed to survive stress.

Your sexually co-dependent roles may not be serving you at this point in your life but you can make good use of the skills and endurance that continue to give them fire. Let's take another look at your sexual needs and see how you can tap into the positive side of your sexual co-dependencies.

Positive Styles Of Sexual Wholeness

Remember the five needs that move women to seek sex? These needs run the gamut from survival to intimacy:

- Economic security
- Positive self-image
- Nurturance
- Power and control
- Pleasure and satisfaction.

Remember also the negative sexual styles that can develop as a result of co-dependency? In the same way, sexual wholeness and cooperation engender their own set of styles and roles. They are positive and they are active. Looked at all together, they read like a Who's Who in a Personals column.

Table 4.1 is very different from Table 2.1 which details negative sexual styles. Is it for real?

Of course it's for real. Just as real as the negative styles. What's important to understand is that reality is complex. You have the potential to activate all these parts inside you.

Each negative co-dependent style has its positive cooperative side. Try this with any of the styles. For instance, if your need is nurturance and your co-dependent style is to kill with kindness and never get any satisfaction in return (**Ms. Goodbar**), you can bet a bundle there's an **Earth Mother** inside you, somewhere, ready to fill you — and your partner — with

Table 4.1. Sexual Wholeness: Women's Needs And Styles

Need	Sexual Style
Economic Security	**Top Banana** assertive exciting imaginative self-responsible able to negotiate
Positive Self-Image	**Magnetic Maggie** attractive irrepressible responsive funny charming
Nurturance	**Earth Mother** sensitive nurturing generous able committed
Power And Control	**Wonder Woman** intense (highly charged) passionate magic playful
Pleasure And Satisfaction	**Gloria Mundi** warm open inviting comfortable intimate
Other	

well-being. Likewise, the needy, pathetic **Poor Little Match Girl** has an **Earth Mother** counterpart.

Let's run through the styles and roles of sexual wholeness, briefly, one by one, comparing them to the negative styles and roles of sexual co-dependency.

Characteristics Of Sexual Wholeness

Economic Security

Top Banana is the positive side of **Forever Amber** and **Shrinking Violet.** **Banana's** need for economic security moves her to develop ingenuity and crackerjack negotiating skills, which help her hold her own in bed, even if her partner can be a sexist bore at times. She is active, assertive, successful, aware of her own needs and able to "read" others. She asks for what she wants and knows how to do this so engagingly that it's a pleasure for her partner to satisfy her. What's more, she knows how to play safe, so her satisfaction doesn't land her with sexually transmitted diseases or unwanted pregnancies. She's exciting, imaginative and energized by her sexual encounters.

Positive Self-Image

Magnetic Maggie is the positive side of **Total Woman** and **Sleeping Beauty.** Her need for positive self-image moves her to actively seek out sexual relationships. Her key quality is *attractiveness* — and that means more than prancing around in a tight skirt or lying around waiting to be discovered. She is loaded with charm. She may not be a classic beauty but she is interested and alive and she looks you in the eye. She feels good and feels good to be around. She beams out such personal magnetism that people automatically move toward her, including potential partners. Her magnetism abounds in her intimate relationships, where she is irrepressible, responsive, funny.

Nurturing

Earth Mother is the positive side of **Ms. Goodbar** and **Poor Little Match Girl.** To fill her need for nurturance, she is loving, generous, sensitive, able and committed. She also takes care of herself as well as others. She's filled with health and well-being. She's also a good sport and likes adventure. She'll try anything at least once and doesn't mind getting dirty. Above all, she is joyful and centered, with warm hands and a big candy heart, like Raggedy Ann's, that says, "I Love You." She hasn't a jealous bone in her body and is greatly turned on by her partner's joy.

Power And Control

Wonder Woman is the positive side of **Big Bertha** and **Hostage Keeper.** She, too, is a bedroom dynamo but she doesn't rage or take hostages. Her needs for power and control make her intense and passionate. She moves fast and can be a playful, inventive lover, with a seemingly inexhaustible supply of sexual energy. Sexual satisfaction is the jet fuel that propels her through the rest of her life, adding to her creative potential. People wonder where she gets her power. Hence the name, **Wonder Woman.**

Pleasure And Satisfaction

Gloria Mundi is the positive side of **Mata Hari** and **Sponge.** She is worldly, with big appetites for pleasure and satisfaction. She pursues them openly and delightfully but she doesn't need to eat a partner alive. She likes all sensations: sun, water, food. She is warm, intimate, inviting and comfortable with her self — body and soul. She understands the art of feeling good. She is mistress of the sensual bubblebath, the playful massage.

How is it possible to move from sexual co-dependence to wholeness and cooperative interdependence? This requires not only self-knowledge but concentration, discipline and commitment.

Steps To Sexual Wholeness

1. **Accept where you are** on your life's map — so that you can begin to find out how to move in the direction you want:

- Recognize your sexual styles — your cooperative styles as well as your co-dependent ones.
- Be aware that you have a variety of needs and you may play more than one part.
- Be aware that you may flip back and forth between co-dependency and wholeness.
- Be aware that different partners or situations may evoke different styles from you. And that you may be different now than you were in the past.

2. **Allow yourself to explore the old feelings** that are still there underneath your defensive co-dependent roles and styles. Beneath the pain are the roots of the vibrant, cooperative, sexual woman you are able to become.

- Acknowledge your sexual defenses, even if you're thoroughly tired of them. Most of them have been in place for many years and have served you well.
- Give yourself time. This process of exploration and discovery is not going to happen overnight.
- Use all the resources that are available to you. Seek out understanding friends and family, self-help groups, therapy. You don't have to go through these old feelings alone.
- Be kind to yourself. Self-exploration is a high-stress activity. So it can also be a chance to learn to take care of yourself — through nutrition, exercise, relaxation — and to plug into positive memories.

3. **Be open to positive change**. As you begin to alter your behavior in the present you may experience a number of shifts in your life and in your sexual relationship. You may even alter your perception of the past.

- You may begin to feel different about yourself. Instead of shame, guilt and hollowness you may begin to feel self-esteem, pride and wholeness.
- Your relationship with your partner may become both clearer and more deeply feeling.

- You may discover childhood memories of warmth and delight lurking beneath memories of neglect and abuse. These positive memories may be fleeting at first and they may even be unbelievable, as if they really belong to someone else. But it's crucial that you own them. Positive memories can greatly enhance your pleasure. They can also become a solid grounding for you in times of stress.

4. **Communicate what's happening** on your journey from sexual co-dependence to sexual wholeness. This doesn't mean you have to spill all your beans (after all, you have a right to privacy) but it may mean giving up habits of compulsive secret-keeping. Talking about what's happening can help make it real. Zipping your lips shut tight is likely to keep your growth and change in the realm of fantasy.

- Keep journals, draw pictures. Talk to yourself. Try it right out loud — to reinforce your own awareness.
- Talk to your partner, if you have a partner. If she or he is on a growth path, there could be a wonderful opening between you. If your partner's entrenched in a co-dependent lifestyle, then trying to communicate your new feelings will feel like rowing through a river of molasses — but at least you'll have an idea of where the relationship bogs down.
- Be open to relationship fallout. Even if your partner is solidly committed to a course of growth, growth means change — and change can rock the relationship boat.

5. **Practice.** These steps can change your life.

Setting The Stage For Sexual Wholeness

Jennifer 2: Moving To Recovery

We have already met Jennifer. Her sexual dysfunction is whole-person disconnection, an all-too-familiar state for women even though it's not listed in the sex therapy literature as a sexual dysfunction. Obsessed with the intercourse that her husband is unable to give her, her co-dependent sexual style swings between the active role of hot demanding **Big Bertha** and the passive role of **Sleeping Beauty**, who is unable to please herself (or even wake herself up).

Jennifer's sexual co-dependency triangle is huge for her right now. She says it influences all aspects of her life to the point where she feels suicidal. All three legs of the triangle are strongly evident: post-traumatic stress, skewed psychosexual development and sex-negative, woman-negative cultural influences.

Jennifer needs help, fast. But where to begin? How is it going to be possible to shift the emphasis for Jennifer so that she can reframe her co-dependency skills into sexual wholeness?

Because Jennifer is an Adult Daughter with a history of double messages about sex, she has no clear sense of the range of sexual normality. To begin to make her transition from sexual co-dependency to sexual wholeness, one essential that Jennifer needs is information. Specifically, she needs information about herself and her own responses. She also needs to know about the possibility of finding a whole person under all that co-dependency.

How is Jennifer going to be able to tap into positive resources from the inside rather than constantly searching outside herself? The task is to find a path she hasn't tried before, perhaps by surprising her.

To help her begin, I asked her to do the following exercise. It's an exercise in imagination. I call it *Seeing Is Believing.* You can try this yourself. It works.

Seeing Is Believing

1. *Close your eyes and breathe.* Take a few deep cleansing breaths and allow your body and mind to let go of any tension they may be holding. Take as much time as you need. This step is important.

As you breathe, find a way to tell yourself that you're about to take a trip into your imagination and that it's okay to accept whatever you find there.

If you encounter any *Shoulds* about how you are supposed to think or feel or behave, greet them politely and tell them you don't need their help right now. Show your *Shoulds* to a waiting room and ask them to sit down there until you are ready to ask for their help again. Then shut the door.

2. *Back to your trip.* Breathe again and imagine yourself going to the video store. There on the rack among the New Releases, you find a video called *Bedroom Scenes.* As you look closer, you discover that the star of this video looks extremely familiar . . . because the star is *YOU.* You realize that you have a unique opportunity to witness *YOU —* making love.

3. *Bring the video home* and slip it into your VCR. Fast forward it to a moment when sex doesn't work — a moment when you're playing a sexually co-dependent role. In Jennifer's case, this is **Big Bertha** or **Sleeping Beauty.** For you, it may be any role we've mentioned so far, or it may be one that is special only to you.

As you watch the video of you in a co-dependent bedroom scene, notice whether or not there is any dysfunction connected with that role — in Jennifer's case, it is whole-person disconnection in conjunction with Martin's impotence.

4. *Become involved.* Whether or not there is specific sexual dysfunction, keep watching as the tape unfolds the story of your sexual co-dependency. When you're ready, let your imagination help you become even more involved in the scene before you. Imagine that you become so involved that you can cross the boundary of reality and step into the video, so that you are actually playing the role now and *feeling* it.

Notice how familiar the role feels. Feel your sexual responses and your partner's. Is there pleasure? Pain? Confusion? Satisfaction? Relaxation? Guilt?

Whatever is there, acknowledge it. Remember, your *Shoulds* are in the waiting room. They aren't around to help you figure out your perceptions.

5. *Flip the tape.* When you have enough information about how it feels to play your co-dependent role, step out of the video and return to the stance of Watcher. As

Watcher, you are aware that there is a flip side to your co-dependent tape, and you know that flip side is sexual wholeness.

Now flip the tape over so that you can watch the reverse side — the side on which you can see yourself as a whole, cooperative, *inter*dependent lover.

You're in charge of the tape. move it around until you come to a scene when you are experiencing sexual ecstasy, bliss or whatever your term is for *The Best.* This may be a time you remember. Or it may be a time you haven't experienced yet but can only imagine.

Watch the scene unfold. What role are you playing here? Notice how you feel as you watch.

When you're ready, let yourself enter into this scene, just as you did on the co-dependent side of the tape. Step inside the video and feel what it's like to make love *exactly the way you want to.* Stay with your experience for a moment, and just enjoy . . .

6. *Become aware.* When you're ready, step outside the scene and begin to be aware which qualities your cooperative self has that make sex feel so good to you. Chances are some of these qualities are the positive ones listed earlier in this chapter.

7. *Choose your Shoulds.* When you've finished watching the tape, remove it from the VCR and take it back to the video store. As you do so, let yourself feel confident that you can check it out again whenever you want.

Before you return to the here-and-now, open the door of the waiting room where you have asked your *Shoulds* to stay. Decide which of them you would like to ask to rejoin you and which you would like to have remain in the waiting room until further notice.

8. *Return.* When you feel ready, wiggle your fingers and toes, open your eyes and come back to the here-and-now.

What was Jennifer's response to this exercise?

Jennifer, who could not remember having experienced love expressed in any other way except intercourse, discovered a new dimension of herself in her imagination. She was able to step beyond the rigid bounds of her childhood version of normality; beyond her triangle of traumatic stress, skewed psychosexual development and sexist cultural heritage. She was able to see the positive side of her sexual co-dependency. For the first time in her life, she was able to imagine herself making love, instead of just having sex.

Here it is in her words:

> I had this extraordinary experience watching myself — as if I was mourning my sexual dreams. What I saw was the sex I never had. In my ecstatic scene I wasn't having an affair with Robert Redford. I wasn't even having intercourse. I was cradled in Martin's arms. I was naked and he was rocking me like a baby. I felt myself begin to sob and I sobbed as if there were no bottom to the tears.
>
> Somewhere in the tears I had this flash of knowledge — a pure knowing all through my being. In that moment I knew that I was not to blame for all the misery in our sexual relationship. And at the same time, I understood that I was in control of what felt good and bad.
>
> I finally saw — I literally saw — that I could change the way I had sex — not by demanding something Martin couldn't give but by understanding that what he couldn't give wasn't my fault. Also I could figure out what I really wanted, which was something Martin could give — warmth and hugging and utter faithfulness.

Transformation And Adjustment

Before closing, it is essential to note the difference between transformation and adjustment. Transforming your sexual co-dependency into sexual wholeness means tapping into your positive possibilities. Adjusting to an unsatisfying sexual situation means putting your own wants and needs aside to comply with your partner's wants and needs and perhaps with your partner's dysfunctions and co-dependencies.

Sexual cooperation doesn't mean compliance and it doesn't mean taking care of your partner's problems. It means knowing who you are so you can deal with sex together. Sex that works for both partners is a two-person process. That means *both* of you have to be fully present in the bedroom at the same time.

For instance, suppose Jennifer had figured out that what she really wanted was something Martin really couldn't give? This would involve both Jennifer and Martin. It would present new crises and bring up needs for new skills, including self-assessment, partner assessment and negotiating. In the words of my irreverent ACoA group, Jennifer and Martin would qualify for the honorable fellowship of AFOG. The initials stand for Another Flipping Opportunity for Growth and we will be dealing with various AFOGs in chapters that follow. Next we will talk about specific ways you can update your old messages and reassess your sexual normality.

❦ FIVE ❦

The Reality Test: Updating Your Old Messages About Sex And Love

Was sex the best kept secret in *your* family? If you were like Bonnie or Sarah the answer is definitely Yes.

Bonnie: Protecting Father

When I was growing up, sex only happened when we were asleep. There were six girls and our father had sex with all of us. But only in the middle of the night. Mother was asleep. And so were the rest of us, even Father.

You think I'm joking. I'm dead serious. They used to joke about our sleepwalking. "You girls are going to fall out the window some-day," they'd say, "and then we'll have to call the police." All my growing-up life I worried about my sleepwalking. I've been married for 18 years now and there's never been a single incident. I finally figured out that sleepwalking was a family joke. A part of the incest scene we all went along with. The myth that we were a perfect family. The myth that protected my father. It went like this:

77

One by one, we girls would "sleepwalk" into the den, where father had "fallen asleep" on the sofa watching TV. Then in his "sleep," father would unzip his pants and put our heads between his legs. Then we would "sleepwalk" back to our beds, wake up in the morning — and "nothing" would have happened. Nobody knew anything. Nobody was responsible.

Sarah 1: Family Denial Of Sex

Sarah's family story is very different from Bonnie's. It concerns a different kind of secrecy about sex — one that can also make for skewed development and lead to dysfunctional relationships. Bonnie told this story during the therapy she sought to save her marriage, which was crumbling because the sex wasn't working.

> If you grew up in my family, you learned that sex didn't exist — not at all. Sometimes I wonder how I got here. I think I must have been an Immaculate Conception. I know for sure I must have been born with all my clothes on.
>
> Of course I went wild when I was a teenager. My parents never knew. They couldn't have even guessed the things I did. How could they? Sex wasn't in their frame of reference.
>
> When I got pregnant they sent me to a home and told everybody I was away at school. They made me give up my baby. She was a little girl. It was all arranged for me and never mentioned again.
>
> Somehow I just turned off sex after that. In fact nothing seemed to be much fun anymore. I spent a couple of years trying to commit suicide and then I married Hal. He's steady and good. He's my best friend but I've never come to orgasm with him. I know he feels passionate about me but I've never been able to feel that way about him.

Skewed Messages

Not all sexual secrecy produces stories that are as dramatic as Bonnie's and Sarah's. And not all unhealthy sexual dynamics in a family center around secrecy. In most families in our culture, messages about sex are simply skewed. They are mixed up with dynamics other than pleasure and satisfaction, such as security, self-worth, nurturance, power and control. If you grew up in a family with skewed messages your lovemaking may be fraught with ghosts.

It's important to add here that not all sexual dynamics in a family are unhealthy. And not all unhealthy sexual dynamics produce full-blown sexual dysfunction. But however your family dealt with sex (or didn't deal with it), strong messages were transmitted nonetheless. These affected how you responded to sex then, and they continue to affect how you respond to sex now. In fact, unless you come to grips with your family's sexual messages, they can affect you for the rest of your life.

How do you begin to update these messages? First, you have to find out what they are. Try this simple formula:

1. Whenever you experience sexual dysfunction — however you define it for yourself — be as aware as you can of exactly how you feel inside. There's an enormous variation of feelings possible; everything from *spacy* to *suicidal* to *wanting to blow up the Western world.*
2. Then, remember a time in your past when you felt the same way — whether that feeling had anything to do with sex or not. One problem you may have is locating the appropriate feeling. Another problem may be that you fear getting lost in the feeling once you've located it; that you may be unable to find your way back to the present.

This device may be helpful in leading you into — and out of — your old feelings. It comes from the ancient world. It's the ball-of-string trick Greek heroes used when tyrants threw them into mazes. They tied one end to the entrance when they went in, and then they could find their way out again by following the string.

Imagine that you are holding a ball of string that leads back to the very center of your past. And imagine that you can follow the string until it leads you back through the maze of your past to the feeling that exactly matches what you're feeling inside yourself now, when you experience sexual dysfunction.

Here's a dialogue from a therapy session to give you an idea:

Carolyn: Connecting Present With Past

Carolyn: I want sex with Charlie so much and what do I do when we go to bed? I argue with him. I berate and badger him for all the things he hasn't done during the day. Then of course he rolls over and goes to sleep because he doesn't want to listen to me and then I cry myself to sleep.

Gina: Where have you felt those feelings before? Follow the string back to the past . . .

Carolyn: When I was married to Dan . . . I'd been trying to get pregnant for years and I was so thrilled to finally have a baby. When she was 10 days old, I found a love letter in Dan's pillowcase. He'd been having this secret affair the whole time I was pregnant. The bottom dropped out of my world.

Gina: You had arguments in bed?

Carolyn: We'd stay up all night arguing and yelling. I was taking care of a new baby. All that going on and no sleep. I went crazy. I tried to slash my wrists. Then I tried to drive the car off a bridge. I finally went to a shrink who put me on Mellaril and of course my milk dried up. Eventually Dan left me and I pasted myself together and went on with my life.

Gina: Without ever resolving those feelings?

Carolyn: Nowhere near resolving them. I never wanted to feel them again. I made a vow to myself.

Gina: I have a hunch that this dynamic of arguing may be attached to something before Dan. Are you willing to follow the string still further back into your past?

Carolyn: . . . I was the peacemaker between my father and mother. I was an only child and my earliest memories are of hearing them fight. Ashtrays and phonebooks whistling through the air. I'd be all alone in my room and I'd cry and scream until I turned blue and then they'd cuddle me and tell me what a good girl I was. Then just as I was getting warm and comfortable they'd go off and leave me and start arguing again. Whenever I wanted them most they'd abandon me — just like my first husband. It happened over and over again . . .

As Carolyn pieced together the painful connections and updated them to her present situation, she understood that they went like this:

Whenever I want closeness and sex or even attention, my old message system kicks in and says I can't have it. What I get instead is endless argument. Argument and loss. Grieving. I've been playing that tape for 37 years. Maybe it's time to play another tune.

Gina: Now follow the string back to the present. Come out of the maze and describe what that new tune might sound like.

Carolyn: Well, I can start by admitting that all this doesn't have much to do with Charlie. I can do something else besides yammer at him when we go to bed. Like nuzzle up to him, or ask for what I want. I can separate out grief from intimacy. I can feel them both but I don't have to feel them both together as the same thing any more.

Carolyn's need for control over the situation is healthy, but it made her a **Big Bertha** in bed. Now she's talking about making the change to **Wonder Woman**. The insight she had may be all she needs to make the transition. But often, women need more than one way to update their messages about sex and love.

Updating Old Messages

To further detox your present sexual relationships, you might need to understand more about the complex maze of your family's sexual attitudes and how your own attitudes came into existence. Here's an exercise I call the Family Message Reality Test.

The questions are designed to help you break through the denial that comes from fear, misinformation or no information at all. They may be questions you've never thought to ask yourself or questions that have been running through your mind for years.

You can tackle them by yourself or with a friend or partner. I have found them extremely effective to ask in a group setting because members are heartened by the information and feed-back from others.

Whether these questions call up old pleasures for you or old pains, they may call up years and years worth of feelings. Allow yourself time to answer thoughtfully — and feelingly. As with other exercises in this book, feel free to add or subtract in order to make this test fit your situation. For instance, there are references to partners and children. If these don't apply to you, respond to the question in the way that works for you.

Family Message Reality Test

1. What were your family's attitudes toward sex when you were growing up? (Note any differences between your father and mother or other parental figures.) _____

2. What are your attitudes towards sex now? _____

3. Do you see any similarity between your sexual attitudes now and those of your family of origin? _____

4. If you have a partner, is your relationship in any way like the sexual relationship between your parents? _____

5. If you have children, do you give them any of the same messages your family gave you? _____

6. What about childhood pleasures like breastfeeding, thumbsucking, cuddling and playing doctor — how were these dealt with in your family? _____

7. What messages did you get about sex when you were an adolescent? _____

8. Were alcohol or other mind-altering substances a part of sex for your parents when you were growing up? _____

9. Have alcohol or other substances been a factor in your sex life? _____

10. Were you sexually abused when you were growing up? Or do you suspect you were sexually abused? Remember, some women have suppressed the direct memory.

_____

11. Did any of the following occur between your parents when you were growing up: separation, divorce, extramarital affairs? _____

12. Were you ever a sexual confidante for either of your parents? _____

13. What kinds of positive sexuality did you see modeled between your parents or other adults in your household (for instance, tenderness, playfulness, passion)? _____

_____

14. Other _____

_____

Finally, if you could sum up your family's attitude toward sex in one word or phrase, what would it be? Some samples from group are:

- Your virginity is your most precious possession.
- Men are out for one thing — sex is dangerous.
- Sex is dirty, save it for the one you love.

Although messages like these may have misinformed and confused you, bear in mind that they may have been delivered out of a realistic concern for your well-being. The world is an unsafe place, especially for little girls and young women.

Some women reported messages that were just plain poison; blatantly negative, angry or sexist:

- Upside down, women are all the same.
- Men are nothing but no-good, rotten bums.

Nonverbal messages can be as powerful as the verbal ones:

In my family I definitely got the message that you could only be affectionate when you were drunk. When you were sober all you expressed was stone-cold anger. This wasn't ever stated, of course, but it was acted out all over the place.

The outcome of this Reality Test is different for everyone. Some find the questions move them to broaden their concept of sex beyond the usual goals of intercourse and orgasm. Others find that directly discussing alcoholism, incest and extramarital affairs takes the taboo out of these subjects and opens up a flood of memories. Still others find they're able to remember positive messages for the first time.

Whatever the specifics, making new connections between past and present can help update old messages about sex and love.

Letter To Your Message-Giver

Okay. Maybe you've got the message. In spite of this, suppose your feelings haven't changed. Suppose nothing's improved when you make love. Now what?

If you find yourself still hooked by the sexual messages you were given when you were growing up, this exercise might be helpful to you:

Write a letter to the early message-giver (or givers) in your life. Because those early messages — and their givers — can evoke such unstructured feelings, structuring the letter can give you a sense of boundaries between past and present and a feeling of general mastery of the situation.

The structure is simply to complete the following thoughts. (Your letter can be as long or short as you like) — and you don't have to send it.

- **I am having the following problem** . . . (describe the problem you are having with your sexual relationship).
- **Here's what I remember getting from you** . . . (describe the sexual messages — the positive ones as well as the negative ones).

- Here's what I've done with it . . . (describe how you used or rejected those early messages to get where you are now).
- Here's what I've decided to do with it in the future . . . (state your intentions for growth and change).
- And furthermore . . . (anything else you feel moved to say).

Here is the letter Sarah wrote to her father, who had been so protective of her virtue and so adamant about her giving her baby up for adoption.

Sarah 2: Letter To Her Father

Dear Dad,

1. I am unable to experience sexual pleasure or give sexual pleasure to my husband, whom I love. I am a tight-ass.

2. Here's what I remember getting from you.

You can't talk intimately to your husband because he will laugh at you. Always keep a frown on your face and don't show affection.

Don't be happy — in particular do not whistle before breakfast. It is unlucky, you will cry before the day is done.

Sex? You can make dirty jokes about it (I remember you and Uncle Josh making lewd remarks about the bodies of lady wrestlers) but what is it? What do you do?

You only marry somebody that is rich.

Do not get seriously interested in anyone unless they are Jewish. Unspoken assumption that the others are "dirty" — somehow contaminated, not clean.

3. Here's what I've done with what I got.

I have become untrusting of others. How can I be trusting when the chief person in my life, who protected me, who was my father, turned on me and hurt me.

I have become unable to feel sexual pleasure.

I have learned to protect myself and my possessions — lock the car everywhere I go — watch where I walk — be careful.

I have internalized much of the crap that you laid on me and started to destroy myself because of my self-hatred and guilt, I was not good enough. I could always be better, I am tense.

4. Here's what I've decided to do with this message in the future. I reject the notion that any men or women are not as good as Jews.

I have decided to open up to people and trust them.

I have decided to become a pleasure-lover — to smell lilacs in the spring, look in the mirror, pamper my body, feel what it's like to walk around the house naked.

I am a good person. I will go out and enjoy myself where, when, how and with anyone I damn please.

5. And furthermore . . . you can take your constant advice and opinions and shove them. And Mom, the same to you!

Sarah did not send this letter to her father, but writing it was a turning point for her. It enabled her to begin her own process of self-forgiveness. Equally important, it allowed her to acknowledge her anger and to place it where it belonged. And it gave her a structure that allowed her to make a strong move from a victim position to active self-acceptance.

I was utterly without power in that situation. Probably they were, too. They were so hooked into what would look good rather than what felt right. All these years I've been taking the responsibility on myself for what happened. Now I'm just plain mad at them. Enraged. But I feel I can deal with that, given time. The point is, I don't have to be mad at me anymore. Somehow I feel freed of that. I don't have to hold on tight anymore. I can let it go and move on.

Your Inner Children In The Bedroom — Elf And Waif

To make the connections between your childhood messages and how you respond sexually as an adult, it may be necessary to graphically remember the sensations of your childhood. That means feeling them.

Actually, that means feeling them *consciously.* These feelings are always there. Whether you're aware of it or not, your inner child climbs in bed with you every time you have a sexual encounter.

Why? Sex involves memories as well as here-and-now stimulation — emotional and spiritual memories as well as physical memories. And these memories are triggered when you are most vulnerable — naked with a partner; sharing your deepest desires, your most essential pleasures. They are present when a tender touch sets off insatiable skin hunger or when your lover sings you a lullaby and you can't stop sobbing.

How do you make those early feelings conscious? You invite your inner child into the bedroom, instead of having her sneak in and hide under the bed. I'm not talking about setting up Inner Incest. I'm talking about acknowledging facts, feelings and connections and bringing them into the light so that you — and your inner child — are in a position of choice about them.

Your inner child is full of old messages about how you should respond sexually. It's time to listen to her — and also to update her.

First of all, consider the notion that you may have more than one inner child. Somewhere inside each woman is an *elf* — playful and bubbling, with snapping eyes and a wide grin. She may be difficult to contact — even more difficult than the *waif* within, the wizened survivor of abuse — because she may be hidden more deeply, more protectively. However, if you want to experience fully integrated sexual desire and satisfaction, you need to be able to invite your *elf* into the bedroom, as well as your *waif.*

Below is a meditation journey designed to help you contact both *elf* and *waif.* Because it's impossible to know which one it will most clearly invoke, this trip can be risky, so be aware that you're in charge and can stop the meditation whenever you want to return to the here and now.

Elf And Waif

Close your eyes and be aware of your breathing. Let the rhythm of your breathing bring you to a path — a path that may be familiar to you. This is the path that leads from far in your future all the way back into your earliest past.

Let your breath lead you down the path back into your past, now, past your adulthood, past your adolescent years, until you come upon a ragged little girl huddled in the dirt. Her eyes tug at your heart. You recognize her as your long-ago abused child of trauma, your inner *waif.*

Invite her to join you on this trip through your past. As you walk with her, ask her about herself. How old is she? What's happening in her life at that age? What are the sexual messages? Take her hand in yours as you walk. Be aware of how it feels to touch your inner *waif.*

Take this opportunity to confide that you know she's around during your sexual encounters in the present, even when she hides under the bed, and that you would like your sexual encounters to be clearer and happier for both of you in the future.

Ask her what she needs from you, as her adult, in order to feel safe when you are in a sexual situation now. Let her answer clearly — and listen with care to her answer.

Tell her what you would like from her when you are in a sexual situation. Be aware of her response. If you need to negotiate with her so that each of you gets what you want, take time to do that now.

When you're ready, notice that a second little girl has joined you. This girl is filled with joy. You can see at a glance that she is interested, alive, aware. She bounces right over to you and introduces herself. She is your inner *elf.* Being near her makes your spirit sing.

Reach out with your other hand to invite her to accompany you and *waif* on your journey into your past. Have the same conversation you just had with her sister *waif:*

- How old is she?
- What's happening in her life?

Notice how it feels to hold her hand. How is this trip different from the trip with her sister *waif?*

- Confide in her about her presence in your sexual experiences.
- Ask how you can help make your sexual experiences safe for her.
- Tell her what you'd like from her when you're in a sexual situation.

When you have said what you want to say to your *elf* and heard her responses, gather both your inner children in your arms. Embrace them. Protect them. Enjoy them. They are your inner family. They are the core of your sexual energy.

Tell them how things are different now — and how some things may be not so different.

Find words they can understand to invite them again into your bedroom. Assure them that you will allow nothing to happen to them while you're making love. Tell them that you're an adult — a loving and sober adult. Tell them that you're in charge while you're making love.

When you know what you can do to make sex safe and good for you *all*, tuck this information in your pocket as you prepare to follow your path back to the here and now. When you feel ready, open your eyes and follow your breathing back to the present, feeling refreshed, aware and knowing you can contact your *waif* and your *elf* again whenever you want.

Once you've contacted your *elf* and your *waif,* it's important to talk about your discoveries with your partner or someone else you trust. This not only validates your experience, but may also offer you additional insight and direction as you seek to update your old messages about sex and love.

This is deep and vulnerable material that lies at the core of your sexuality. Pick a person who will understand. The key word here is *Trust.*

Finding Out What's Normal

If you grew up in a dysfunctional home, you may not know what normal is; you may have to guess. And when you have questions about sexuality, this makes normal doubly hard to understand because society gives women such conflicting messages about sex.

Normal for women may be a broader concept than you think. Remember, normal does not necessarily mean sex is safe or exactly the way you want it to be or even the way that might best further your recovery. It means the way things *are* for women because of biology, family, society and, yes, the individual choices women have made.

- Sexually normal can mean many partners and a very wide range of sexual experience.
- Sexually normal can mean one partner and a very narrow range of sexual experience.
- Sexually normal can mean not having a partner — and not having had a partner, ever.
- Sexually normal can mean experiencing sex differently from the way the media or the scientific books say you

should. Or experiencing it differently from the way your partner expects you to.

- Sexually normal can mean emotional, intellectual and spiritual responses as well as physical responses.
- Sexually normal can mean wanting different kinds of pleasure than your partner does.
- Sexually normal can mean that sex isn't pleasurable for you.
- Sexually normal can mean being afraid of pleasure as well as being afraid of pain.

Here are some questions I am asked repeatedly — and answers that may help you update some of your old messages about sexual normality.

Questions And Answers About Sexual Normality

1. *Is it all right to want too much sex?*

It depends on what you mean by "too much." If it's a question of giving yourself permission to enjoy pleasure and passion, go for it! Liking sex is healthy and normal — even if your partner, your mother, your church or synagogue have told you it's greedy, trashy or immoral.

If "too much" means you're worried that sex is out of control in your life, that you're hurting yourself or others by your sexual actions, then it's time to take a look at how you're using sexuality. Understanding yourself is the first step to helping yourself feel comfortable about sex.

2. *Is it okay to want commitment first?*

Yes, especially in this age of AIDS, where it may be literally worth your life to have a partner who cares about your health and well-being — a partner you know you can trust not to give you a sexually transmitted disease.

Emotional safety is also a factor. For some women commitment is an essential ingredient of great sex, allowing them to let go into their most intimate feelings. For others, it is quite the opposite; the whole idea of commitment is so scary that the juices stop flowing.

The most important thing to do is to make sure you know what the terms of the commitment are and that you agree with them. Commitment can be a loaded concept, harkening back to its old meaning of traditional marriage, with all the trappings that have ensnared so many women. If this is what commitment means to you or your partner, then it's a prime set-up for sexual co-dependency.

Whatever your degree of commitment, make sure it goes both ways. It's easy for some women to focus on taking care of their partners and to forget about themselves. Remember, you're important too. It's okay to play **Earth Mother,** but **Total Woman** leaves your needs untended.

3. *If I'm disgusted by certain sexual practices, does that make me a prude?*

Give yourself credit for having good reasons for what you like and what you don't like. That way, you can stand up for your tastes — or decide to make changes.

There is such variety in women's sexual tastes that it is impossible to arrive at a strict definition of what's normal. For instance, some women are disgusted by fellatio (giving oral sex to a man). What are their reasons?

- They don't know what's expected of them.
- Their partner hasn't had a bath.
- They're afraid their partner will ejaculate in their mouth.
- Oral sex restimulates memories of childhood sexual abuse.

To talk about reasons like these in an honest and feeling way can create enough understanding to change the whole tone of your sexual attitude — and your partner's. Remember, sex is an exploration you do together. You don't have to be a **Shrinking Violet** and do what your partner wants just because he wants you to do it. And that's true if your partner's a woman, too.

If your partner insists on sexual practices that disgust you, even after you have been clear about your preferences, that might be a hint to take a long hard look at your total relationship.

4. *Suppose I'm bored out of my tree?*

If you're bored, listen to your boredom. It could be a bridge to a healthier and more interesting relationship with yourself and with your partner.

Are you spending enough relaxed time together? Are you getting the kind of stimulation that turns you on — intellectual and emotional, as well as physical? It's important to tune up your sexual partnership from time to time. It can't run forever without attention, any more than your car can.

Sexual boredom may indicate more than that it's time to change the spark plugs. It may mean you're turning off the whole relationship. Re-examination of your relationship and of the roles you play in it might be in order.

Sexual boredom may also be a sign that you need to do some self-examination. Maybe you've changed and your partner has stayed the same. Maybe you *haven't* changed, but are ready to. Maybe boredom is really the denial phase of something else — like anger or fear.

Sexual boredom may be more than just a bore. If you can't get a handle on your sexual boredom, find some help.

5. *What if I have a physical disability?*

Having a physical disability doesn't mean you can't enjoy sex — emotionally, spiritually or physically. There may be logistics that you need to deal with and these may be profound, depending on your degree of disability. There may be information you need (see the bibliography for resources). You may have to learn to deal with other people's notion that you're not a sexual being. You may also need to deal with self-image problems of your own.

One thing to bear in mind is that in this pleasure-negative, woman-negative culture, we're all sexually disabled. Your own attitudes about sex may be more enlightened than others'.

6. *What if I like making love to women?*

You're not alone. This is normal for an estimated 10 to 15 percent of the women in this country. Some women are born knowing they love women. Others come to this awareness over a period of time, often after one or more heterosexual relationships.

Whether or not you identify yourself as a lesbian, there are many advantages in being a woman who loves women. One is that you don't have to put up with sex differences — and sexist differences — in and out of bed. Another is that you are in the lowest risk category for sexually transmitted diseases, including AIDS.

But there can be drawbacks, too — mainly prejudice. Socially, you are part of an invisible minority. You may be forced to keep your relationship closeted in order to keep your job, your children, your home. Being part of a positive women's community can help you feel a sense of belonging.

Don't let anyone tell you you are sick or perverted if you love women. And don't let anyone try to "help" you change. Your sexual orientation is basically a matter of preference, just as it is for heterosexuals.

7. *Is it normal to experience something beyond orgasm — something called ecstasy?*

Yes. Many women who have talked with me find that descriptions of physical orgasm don't begin to touch what they feel during their peak sexual experiences. What they describe is a flowing together of body and soul, mind and emotions. They describe the feeling as *connecting, at peace, melting.* They also report that such experiences change their sexual responses (and other responses) long after the sexual encounters are over. I call this the Ecstasy Connection.

Let me add here that it's also normal *not* to experience this Ecstasy Connection — or not to experience it as a result of sex. In other words, please don't take other women's experience to stand as a goal that you have to strive for and achieve in order to feel normal.

8. *Do I deserve it?*

If by "it" you mean sexual pleasure — the answer is Yes! Update your internal sexual message center and believe you deserve it. Because if you don't believe you deserve pleasure, you can't expect your partner to.

Sexual Normality Chart

This is a chart on which you can map your own sexual responses and see exactly where they come from and the memories they trigger. There's a 20-point range. Minus numbers are for the sensations you don't like and plus numbers are for the ones you do.

As you make your list, be sure you include emotional items as well as physical ones. For instance, you might say your partner's drinking beer and making sex jokes gets a minus six but your partner nuzzling your ear may get an eight and looking into your eyes and saying, "I love you" goes off the chart.

The purpose of this chart is to provide an honest, timely self-assessment of your physical and emotional tastes, your sexual orientation and your readiness for sexual growth. Above all, it invites you to define for *yourself* what sexual normality is — and how much pleasure you deserve.

Feel free to change it to fit your situation — and to fill out separate charts for separate relationships, if that seems relevant.

When you've completed this chart, notice what, if anything, you'd like to change about your sexual response.

Chart 5.1. Sexual Normality Chart

Sexual Experiences I Enjoyed	How Much I Enjoyed Each Experience	Memories Triggered By Each Experience
	-10 -8 -6 -4 -2 0 2 4 6 8 10	
Physical		
Emotional		
Intellectual		
Spiritual		

❖‖ SIX ‖❖

The ABCs Of Healthy Sexual Communication

Jackie asks: But how do I begin? How can I bring it up without scaring my partner? What words do I use? How do I know it's the right moment? It's a lot easier to have sex than it is to talk about it!

Jackie's concerns are typical for women in recovery. Sex is hard for almost every woman to talk about in a whole way because there are so many societal messages that say *Don't Talk* — almost as if it's a matter of life and death. And most women have no role models to follow. Your mother and grandmothers, for instance, were closer to the repressive Victorian era and were probably silenced about sex much more than you are today.

In addition, no matter how successful you are in the struggle to update your childhood messages and clear yourself from your sexually co-dependent styles, you and your partner are likely to remain mired in unhappy old dynamics unless you are both able to communicate clearly. Communication affects your sexual health, your sexual relationship — even your potential sexual relationship. Some experts go so far as to say that sex *is* communication.

How can you focus on your partner without sliding back down the thorny path of sexual co-dependency? And how can you communicate your own sexual concerns and desires, when you're taught to believe that good girls are to be seen but not heard?

What do you say after you say hello? Just how far should you go? And how fast? How do you move beyond the five-finger exercise stage of talking about sex into the nitty-gritty of sexual desire, entitlement amd safety?

This chapter will guide you through the ABCs of healthy sexual communication: what to talk about with a partner and how to talk about it; how to move beyond talk to body language. It may also guide you beyond body language to that mysterious language of the imagination.

Notice that I'm not offering you a whole alphabet soup here, just the first few letters. These are based on your understanding of cooperative sexual interdependence and the sexual messages you received in childhood.

Verbal Communication: Talking About Sex

Exactly *what* do you talk about? There are some subjects that all women eventually need to be able to share with their partners in the interests of moving beyond sexual co-dependency and towards sexual cooperation. These are:

- Sexual safety
- Sexual needs
- Early sexual messages
- Body image
- Whole-self image
- Sexual fears
- Sexual tastes
- Sexual self-pleasure
- Sexual dreams and fantasies.

If you feel overwhelmed at the prospect of having to bring up all these subjects, relax. In the first place, you don't have to talk about them all at once. And secondly, you can choose your time and place to begin.

Let's look at these subjects one by one.

Sexual Safety

This is an absolute must in this age of AIDS and other sexually transmitted diseases such as herpes and chlamydia — unless you want to end up like **Shrinking Violet**, selling out your health for the sake of not making waves in the bedroom. But safe sex can mean much more than freedom from disease, it can mean sex that's emotionally and spiritually safe, too — dealing with the co-dependency connections.

In *Safe Encounters* Beverly Whipple and I offer a golden rule that spells S-A-F-E. It suggests ways to communicate about safe sex. It applies to sex with women as well as sex with men:

Slow down.

Ask questions.

Feel good about yourself (your self-image, your rights).

Exercise your right to safe sex (that is, be active in your own behalf).

With a new or potential partner it's crucial that you understand exactly how safe sex works and that you're clear about your sexual rights. Even in a monogamous marriage, the ability to bring up the subject of safe sex might save your life. For more information on sexual safety, see chapter 8. For a detailed guide to the how-to's, read *Safe Encounters.*

Your Sexual Needs

Talking about your needs is a way to develop intimacy as well as to check out your partner. Remember, everyone has needs that move them to seek sexual relationships. Earlier we listed five needs: economic security, positive self-image, nurturing, power and control, pleasure and satisfaction.

Talk about how you get hooked in sexual relationships and how you hook partners. You can use examples of negative roles in Table 2.1. Together, you can figure out which ones you're likely to play. Together, you can talk about how to activate the interdependent roles.

Let's give a sample dialogue: Marcia has decided to tell Mel that she'd like to be warm and fuzzy, a sensual comfort lover (a potential **Gloria Mundi**), but that her passive dependency in the form of **Sponge** gets in the way, aided by neediness (**Match Girl**) and depression and immobility (**Sleeping Beauty**).

Marcia: Breaking The Ice

Marcia: You know how you wish I'd take showers with you?
Mel: Mm-hmmm.
Marcia: And you know how I'm always too tired?
Mel: Mm-hmmm.
Marcia: Well, it isn't that I don't want to take showers with you. It's that I get into wanting you to take care of me.
Mel: Mm-hmmm?
Marcia: So what I'm trying to say is that I have some very real needs about being taken care of because I missed out on so much when I was little. But I also want to be warm and intimate and grown-up with you.
Mel: So what are you saying about the sexy showers?
Marcia: I'm saying it would be an incredible turn-on for me if you would make the arrangements instead of expecting me to. You know, clean up, make the bathroom nice, maybe light a candle.
Mel: You mean you want me to take care of you?
Marcia: Yeah, I guess I am saying that. But not all the time. What I'm really saying is that I'd like you to help take care of *us*. I want you to recognize that I have a need for some caretaking before I can feel open enough to feel sexual. And if you can do that — like the candle and maybe clean towels — then I can act more like a grown-up instead of wanting to crawl under the covers and go to sleep.
Mel: So all I have to do is set things up and you'll hop in the shower with me and not be tired?
Marcia: That's a start.
Mel: Sounds good to me.

This was only a beginning to the communications Marcia and Mel were to have over the next years. But it was a significant exchange because it broke the sexual ice that had formed between them.

Your Early Sexual Messages

What were they? Who were the message-givers? Which messages have you each decided to incorporate into your present value system? Which have you decided to give up? If you wrote a letter to your message-giver, reading it to your partner might be an ideal way to introduce your responses to your early messages.

How do you transform these messages into something that can have a positive effect on your sexuality? Let's listen to Becky.

Becky: Exorcising The Harpies

Becky realized that the sexual fears her mother and aunt had instilled in her were undermining her pleasure in sex.

> It was as if those women were Harpies and they were there in bed with me telling me what to do. Or more likely, telling me what not to do.

She decided to become **Wonder Woman** and throw the Harpies out of the bedroom. But she decided to do it in a cooperative way, and enlist the help of her lover.

> I told Chris what I wanted to do and asked her if she'd help me put some humor into the effort. I get decidedly humorless when dealing with Mother and Aunt Merle. So she suggested waiting until the full moon and then making as much ruckus in the bedroom as we could.
>
> The most fun was talking about it beforehand. For instance, we couldn't make too much noise because we didn't want to scare the neighbors. So we had to figure out silent ways to do it. We made elaborate plans and giggled a lot.
>
> The actual night of the full moon was kind of anti-climactic. We shook the sheets and waved our arms around. But, you know, even before we did it, I think those women were out of there for good. The real exorcism wasn't our dancing around in the full moon. It was all that talking about it beforehand.

Your Body Image

What do you each like about your bodies? Talking about the positives may be excruciatingly hard if you've been physically abused or brainwashed into thinking your body is garbage. But think of the benefits. It can be a wonderful exercise in self-assertion, letting your partner know that you think your body is important.

What do you dislike about your bodies? This may be important to talk about, too. Not to give each other ammunition for put-downs, but to let each other know exactly where you're sensitive and where you may need help enhancing your body image. The list of negatives may be endless once you get going. After all, the media image of sexy is young, sleek, agile, sweet-smelling and proportioned "perfectly." Women, especially, tend to get down on themselves for falling short of this ideal and find themselves . . .

- Too fat
- Too skinny
- Too hairy
- Too smelly
- Too old
- Too different.

"Too different" can be especially tough to bear — and talk about — if you have physical disabilities, if you've had a mastectomy, if you're not orgasmic, if your skin is the "wrong" color — if, if, if . . . (you complete the sentence). But if you can communicate your feelings to a partner, at least you don't have to carry them around inside you anymore.

Chances are, your partner accepts you even if you can't quite accept yourself. And if not, well, it's probably easier on you to find out now than when you're already deeply invested in the relationship. If you already *are* deeply invested in a long-term relationship in which you've never talked about body image, it can be an immense relief to get your unsayable negatives out on the table. If your partner is lovingly supportive, you have deepened your chances for intimacy. If there's friction or lack of support, your honesty may have brought you closer to understanding what direction to take in that relationship, including what help to seek.

Your Whole-Self Image

Sex is more than physical. What do you like about your personality? What do you dislike? Again, it may be harder to talk about positives than negatives, but it's important to talk about both. This may be another time to mention co-dependent roles — and let your partner know your ideas on the cooperative kind of sex you would like. Are you a killer caretaker **Ms. Goodbar**, who'd rather be a nurturing and self-nurturing **Earth Mother**? What would it take to make that transition for you? How could your partner help?

I cannot emphasize too strongly the importance of whole-self image, especially for Adult Daughters, who constantly struggle with questions about their adequacy or even the validity of their existence.

To illustrate the need for whole-self validation, here's a quote from a therapy session with Martin and Jennifer, who we have already met. Jennifer admitted to Martin:

> I need you to tell me you love me. All of me. You could slither all over me covered in almond oil and if you didn't say "I love you" I'd respond like a dead trout.

Your Sexual Fears

It is crucial for you and your partner to understand your own fears and each other's. Otherwise you may put yourself in situations that restimulate old fears.

Tara: Using The Media As An Ally

Tara relates how her role of **Shrinking Violet** served to perpetuate her fear of sex — and her physical dysfunction of vaginismus:

> Whenever my husband came near me I would literally clench up. I was so scared that it was five years before we ever had

intercourse. Our first child was born by artificial insemination. I just couldn't open up to him and I couldn't tell him why. I was afraid he'd leave me if I told him I'd been molested.

Tara needed to talk with her husband but she also needed help getting started. What finally got her conversation flowing was a TV special on incest. Tara let the media be her ally. She also could have used books, newspapers, magazines and films.

It was like thawing after all that cold and tightness. It was such a relief to tell. I see it as the real beginning of our marriage — at least the sexual part. It's going to be a long time before I feel normal. Maybe I'll never feel completely normal. But at least we both speak the same language now and I'm not afraid he's going to leave me.

Your Sexual Tastes

Here we come to the nitty-gritty. Exactly what do you like in bed — and what do you dislike? Both women and men have been trained to think about sex in terms of the genitals and intercourse, so that's what most people imagine they have to talk about first.

Think for a moment though about all the sexual possibilities there are. Every part of your body is potentially erotic — fingers and toes and ears as well as genitals. Intercourse is actually only a small part of sex. There is a whole sexual world beyond, and that is called *outercourse*.

Outercourse As Well As Intercourse

Outercourse means everything *but* intercourse. It is overall body pleasure together with the emotional, spiritual and relational aspects of making love. Outercourse is usually more appealing to women than to men, at least at first, until women have trained their male partners away from the goal-oriented race for the "real thing" and into a slower, more flowing form of making love. I realize this may not be true for all women in all their sexual encounters, but in my clinical experience most women say that what would enliven their sex lives is more outercourse and less emphasis on intercourse.

If you are an Adult Daughter who's confused about what normal is, it may be important for you to hear that outercourse is perfectly normal sex. It just hasn't had the same degree of press coverage as intercourse.

In any event women tend to be more turned on by the emotional, spiritual and relational aspects of making love, which are nonphysical aspects of outercourse.

So when you think about communicating your sexual tastes, remember outercourse as well as intercourse. If you want to know more about it, see chapter 3 of *Safe Encounters*.

Sexual Self-Pleasure

There are many taboos about masturbation, so this may be hard to talk about at first, but talking about how you masturbate can really pay off. For starters, taking the risk is likely to raise the intimacy ante between you and your partner. Second, letting your partner know how you pleasure yourself — or how scared you are to pleasure yourself — can provide valuable information about your sexual responses.

Some hot tips on how to bring this subject up:

- Get a book on self-stimulation (*For Yourself* is a good one) and underline the parts you'd like your partner to read.
- Gather some of your favorite masturbation myths and giggle about them together. Do you *really* have hair on your palms? Did your priest *really* have X-ray vision so he could tell when you were "abusing" yourself?
- Start with the least threatening self-pleasures and progress toward those that are scarier to mention. For instance, it may be a sensual treat for you to eat an ice cream cone, skinny-dip in the ocean, wear silky fabric next to your skin. If you can start by talking about pleasures like these, it may pave the way for talking about how it feels to touch your skin with your fingers. And that, in turn, may

pave the way for talking about touching your own breasts, clitoris and vagina.

Sexual Dreams And Fantasies

Here's another taboo you can break through. If you were brought up in the traditional American value system, you've probably learned that women aren't supposed to have sexual fantasies and dreams. And if you read scientific books, at least some of them will tell you that women don't fantasize. This can leave you feeling either immoral or abnormal if your daydreams or nightdreams are hopping with sexual imagery.

First, you need to know that the spectrum of normality is very broad here. At one end of the spectrum are those women whose imaginations don't include much sex. At the other end are those who have rich and varied sexual dreams and fantasies.

Sharing your dreams is one of the activities that promotes intimacy. Sharing your sexual dreams is likely to bring you closer together. And remember, whatever you decide to share with your partner, you don't have to share it all at once. Great lovers are allowed to have boundaries.

In learning your ABCs of sexual communication, always bear in mind that it's not only *what* you say, it's *how* you say it. If you come on trumpeting like **Big Bertha**, you may scare a partner away. If you whine like **Shrinking Violet** or **Sponge**, you won't promote an open, two-way conversation.

The great sexual communicators are the sexually coopera-tive roles — **Top Banana, Magnetic Maggie, Earth Mother, Wonder Woman**, and **Gloria Mundi**. As you learn to activate these parts of yourself, you will elicit their help.

Six Guidelines For Effective Verbal Communication

1. **Know your facts.** Whether the subject is self-image or safe sex, take time to know what you want to convey so you don't find yourself fumbling for words.
2. **Speak directly.** Don't hint around hoping your partner will bail you out. For instance, if you want to discuss

masturbation, it may confuse the issue if you refer to it, *That Thing* or *Down There*. Go ahead and use the word *Masturbation* (or *Self-Pleasure* or *Playing With Myself*). Back up and try saying these words now. Form them with your lips. Okay, now try saying them *out loud*. Did a bolt come down from the heavens and strike you dead? If not, read on.

3. **Share personal values.** Sexual cooperation is about values. Values are different from judgments. Values don't put down your partner for having tastes or feelings that are different from yours. Sharing your values states where *you* are — in a way that allows your partner to respond.

4. **Share personal feelings.** Central to sexual cooperation is the flow of feeling between you and your partner. Whether the feelings are present ones or ones from your past, being aware of them and letting your partner know about them will deepen the intimate connections between you.

5. **Be explicit in asking for what you want.** Vagueness does not promote sexual cooperation or satisfaction. Being explicit may mean risking rejection but it also raises the chances that you will get what you want.

6. **Keep it simple.**

For some women, following these steps might involve great courage. If this is true for you, where will you get that courage? You can create courage from practice: Try writing out your thoughts and feelings before testing them on a partner. Then you can read what you've written to yourself — silently at first, then out loud. Need more courage still? Tape yourself reading out loud and listen to the tape until the words become familiar enough so they're not so scary.

Nonverbal Communication: Your Sexual Body Language

Sexual communication goes far beyond words. You communicate as much by what you *don't* say as by what you *do* say, maybe even more. Eye contact or lack of it, smiles or frowns — these are part of the mating dance. Your stance and gestures — are they open or closed, active or passive? These can speak eloquently about your sexual feelings about yourself and toward your partner. How you dress or how you touch your partner can say more about your sexual willingness than any words can tell. Are you poured into a tight black number with your arms draped around your partner's neck or are you clad in your old green robe, weakly plucking at your partner for support?

It doesn't take a Ph.D. in Communications to read signals like these. It doesn't even take the wisdom of years. Children are adept at reading body language. And children from dysfunctional families are particularly adept. They may have developed special sensitivity as part of the survival skills they needed to get through the day without getting clobbered.

If you grew up in a dysfunctional family, you probably grew up with more sensitivity to others than to yourself, and you probably learned to adapt your body language to that of others, regardless of what you felt inside. For example, when you saw your father drinking and beginning to sweep his hands around in expansive gestures, you knew that abusive gestures were soon to follow. You may have made yourself as small and inconspicuous as possible, even though what you were feeling inside was a volcano's worth of rage.

What does this have to do with your sexual communication now? That old survival skill of showing one thing when you're feeling another may mean you're unaware of some of the nonverbal messages you give. Combine that with your learned supersensitivity to others and your learned disconnection from your own feelings, and you have a set-up for the kind of nonverbal sexual communication that fosters sexually co-dependent roles.

Mixed Nonverbal Signals

For an example of how nonverbal signals can convey just the opposite of what you want let's look at **Poor Little Match Girl**. It's nearing the holidays and she's feeling particularly needy. One thing she knows would feel terrific is an evening at home with her partner. Maybe a little music to accompany some slow, sweet lovemaking. She has this expectation all worked out in her head. She really needs this evening though she's waited until she's at the breaking point before admitting it to herself.

How does she express this expectation? She's the one in the old green robe, plucking pathetically at her mate's shoulders. She may be feeling sexy but she's not giving out sexy signals. She's giving out Take Care of Me signals. Only a totally insensitive partner or a partner crazed with lust could disregard such a strong nonverbal message of need and respond with a sexual advance.

Suppose an insensitive or lust-crazed advance ensues. Then **Match Girl**, who is supersensitive to others, could certainly interpret this sexual advance as too much. She might even experience it as rape. And rightfully so, for the sexual advance would be a violation of boundaries. It would have nothing to do with the signals she was sending out.

The upshot is that whether **Match Girl** ends up having sex or not, she won't get what she wants. This will be another messed-up communication that will leave her feeling needier and more unsure of herself than before.

Guidelines For Effective Nonverbal Communication

Now let's talk about effective nonverbal communication, the kind that fosters interdependent sexual cooperation. It starts with straightening out the communication lines within yourself and includes self-sensitivity, self-acceptance, and willingness to question the feedback you're getting. These are all principles we've been talking about throughout the book, so let's go over them only briefly here.

1. **Self-sensitivity.** Knowing what you are feeling is the first step in effective nonverbal communication of any kind. Nobody's perfect in this department, especially about sexual feelings, because of cultural taboos against wom-

en's sexual pleasure and cultural expectations about how women are supposed to respond sexually. An important goal for yourself here might be to develop self-sensitivity not all at once but inch by inch.

2. **Self-acceptance.** Once you've connected up your inner wiring, can you believe what you are feeling? Can you acknowledge it to yourself? Can you welcome it? If so, self-acceptance will shine through your being. People will say, "You look great — you look *different!*" And as if by magic, you may find yourself getting more of what you want sexually.

3. **Questioning feedback.** All communication involves feedback. It's important to find out if the sexual feedback you're getting fits your nonverbal messages.

For instance, are you getting unsexual feedback because you're giving out Take-Care-of-Me **Match Girl** type messages? Or are you getting skewed feedback even though your messages are perfectly clear? I think these are essential questions to ask, because women are often encouraged to take the blame if sex goes away. This is the Eve Syndrome, mentioned earlier in chapter 1.

If you have a partner who's willing to engage with you in self-exploration, you can fine-tune the feedback loops between the nonverbal messages you give and the feedback you get. For instance, Jennifer, whose struggles you have followed in the last two chapters, is able to look back on the positive side of those struggles.

Jennifer 3: Getting Closer

Sure, this period has been painful but it's felt like birth pains, not like a broken leg. Martin and I are closer than we've ever been. Closer than we could have imagined even when we were young and in love.

We're learning every day to rely more and more on our own feelings — to trust ourselves and each other. Now here's a strange nonverbal sexual message. Ever since we moved into this house, Martin has promised he'd fix the kitchen door. Well, one Saturday last month he fixed it. And I knew — I knew right down in my bones — that we would start having some joy back in our sex. Because Martin was finally feeling good enough about himself to come through with his promises.

Do's And Don'ts Of Nonverbal Sexual Communication

Here are some graphic examples of nonverbal sexual communication. One kind is active, straightforward and frankly sexual. The other is convoluted and likely to provoke sexual fights or other uproars. I've called them the Do's and Don'ts of nonverbal sexual communication.

See next page for Do's and Don'ts Chart.

Recovering Your Breath And Your Imagination: More Tools For Sexual Communication

Terry Says:

I feel flat and stomped on, like a circus tent before it's been raised. I can't seem to get up off the ground so the fun can begin.

This is an invitation for you to raise the tent and join the circus. An invitation to breathe, to communicate with yourself and to move through the toxically co-dependent aspects of your sexuality — and your life — by consciously recovering your capacity for air.

Conscious Breathing

Conscious breathing gives you control over a vital function. Breathing is something no one else can do for you and something you can do for no one else. As you become aware of your ability to breathe, each breath can remind you that you are depending on you and you alone — more than 10,000

Do's And Don'ts Of Nonverbal Sexual Communications

DO . . . (Cooperative Communication)	DON'T . . . (Co-dependent Communication)
(**Top Banana**) . . . Take your partner's hand and put it exactly where you want to be stimulated.	(**Forever Amber**) . . . Play footsie with the school principal during the PTA meeting. (**Shrinking Violet**) . . . Shudder when your partner cuddles up to you but not tell why.
(**Magnetic Maggie**) . . . Make positive eye contact with your partner and smile from your heart.	(**Total Woman**) . . . Greet your alcoholic mate at the door in a low-cut negligee and with a martini. (**Sleeping Beauty**) . . . Lie totally still during lovemaking and not tell why.
(**Earth Mother**) . . . Pick up the lobster tail, scoop out the meat with your fingers and feed it tantalizingly to the person you love most.	(**Ms. Goodbar**) . . . Try to turn on your mate by reading a sex therapy manual — looking for his or her dysfunction. (**Poor Little Match Girl**) . . . Wear an old brown sweater to the dance and shake your head when your partner says, "Let's Boogie."
(**Wonder Woman**) . . . Rub your magic bracelet and climb on top.	(**Big Bertha**) . . . Push your mate out of bed, then flounce onto your own side, pouting when you don't get the sex you wanted. (**Hostage Keeper**) . . . Pretend you're wearing a diaphragm.
(**Gloria Mundi**) . . . Draw a warm bath big enough for two. Reach out to your lover in an invitation to join you.	(**Mata Hari**) . . . Park your camper in your new lover's office parking lot and hang out a laundry line with lover's clothing in full view. (**Sponge**) . . . Sob until your lover agrees to stay home from work . . . again.

times a day — for the ongoing, complex job of taking in oxygen and emptying out carbon dioxide.

In addition, conscious breathing can help restore a full range of feeling. This range may have been lost during infancy when as a terrified baby (or neglected, battered or starved baby) you learned that you had one measure of control over your life. You could stop yourself from feeling simply by holding your breath.

Each breath today can remind you of those feelings if you allow it to. Each breath can help you embrace present feelings in your life. Conscious breathing is inspirational, in its most personal and literal sense. Among other things, it can lead you to begin to claim and reclaim your sensuality. You can turn the humdrum job of breathing into an art. Breathing can be a part of integration, joy and pleasure. Breathing can allow sexual satisfaction. Breathing can retain sexual satisfaction, breathing can transform sexual satisfaction into physical and spiritual energy.

A cautionary note: Unlocking your breathing can open up a flood of feelings. Starting slowly will help you be in control of the process. Remember, if conscious breathing stimulates memories that are too painful, you have a safeguard. You can hold your breath for a moment if you want to stop feelings.

Reclaiming Your Breath

Here are four ways to reclaim your breath:

1. **Evoke your breath through exercise.** This awakens and enlivens numbed parts of your body, mind and emotions. Aerobics, walking, swimming or even beating pillows to get rid of aggression can make your breath move faster. The key word here is *conscious.* You are using exercise for awareness instead of avoidance. No amount of huffing and puffing can help you with sexual co-dependency if you are running away from your feelings. In fact, exercising can become an addiction in itself instead of a way through your sexual co-dependency.

2. **Follow your breath into meditation.** This can awaken and enliven your imagination. A meditative state can slow down your flight from feeling and connect you with what is going on inside you. It does this by temporarily dissolving inner boundaries, or defenses, so that you can make connections between body, mind, emotions and spirit that allow you to feel pleasure fully and take it into your whole being.

3. **Celebrate your breath by making noise.** Joyful noises, angry noises, grunts — any of these may express your state of being. So many women have grown up in homes where they were to be seen and not heard, especially if they grew up in homes of trauma. When you make these noises out loud instead of keeping them inside, you are announcing that you have a right to be alive.

   Chanting is a wonderful way to let your breath lead you into feeling — and sometimes through the feelings to a more powerful state. A simple OM is a good place to begin (the actual sound is three syllables: Ahh — Ohh — Ooom). Take a deep breath and "OM" it out loud — by yourself or with others. Chanting your name can bring up feelings, too. For deep effect, try chanting your girlhood name or nickname.

4. **Attune your breath with a partner's.** No, this is not an exercise in sexual co-dependency. It's an exercise in the positive dance of relationship. Try the following exercise to help you practice this dance.

Breathing Together

Sit opposite each other cross-legged on the floor — or however is most comfortable for you.

Close your eyes and breathe until you are each aware of your own internal rhythm.

Now open your eyes and look into each other's eyes — maintaining the rhythm of your breathing and at the same time starting to breathe in sync with your partner. If both of you do this, neither one of you has to give over your own rhythm to take on that of your partner. If you feel yourself losing your own rhythm, simply close your eyes until you regain it, then make eye contact with your partner again.

This may be as much of the exercise as you want to do. And this is a wonderful way to begin lovemaking — to be in touch with both yourself and each other. If you want to extend the exercise, read further.

When you are maintaining eye contact and breathing comfortably and in sync, you are each going to have a series of visualizations about each other. Feel free to substitute others for the ones listed below. The important point is to keep breathing and to maintain eye contact and concentration. Don't talk. Don't make judgments or try to figure the images out as you go along. There'll be plenty of time for sharing at the end.

It helps to have a third person give you the directions so you can concentrate on your breathing, eye contact and visualizations, but if there are only two of you, you can agree on how to do this for yourselves. By the way, this is a dynamite exercise to do in group (the partners in the exercise don't have to be partners in real life).

Take about a minute for each visualization. That means there'll be a lot of silence.

Communicating Through Imagination

First see your partner as an animal. Looking into your partner's eyes, let an image of an animal come into your mind — any kind of animal, large or small. Be aware of the details of the animal, and keep consciously breathing and looking into your partner's eyes as you notice how the animal moves . . .

Next see your partner as a plant. Still looking into your partner's eyes and breathing in sync, imagine the shape of the plant and the color and how it grows . . .

Now see your partner as a landscape. Look all around so you can see 360 degrees. What kind of a landscape is it — country or city? Is it brightly colored or muted? Learn how it feels to move around in this landscape that is your partner . . .

Now see your partner as a kind of weather. Stormy, clear and radiant — whatever kind of weather you see, keep breathing and keep looking into your partner's eyes . . .

See your partner, now, as a famous lover. Perhaps a lover out of history, perhaps a surprise lover you've never heard of. See in detail what the lover is doing. Be aware what the important qualities are that make this lover so renowned . . .

See your partner as a young person — a child, maybe even a tiny baby. See what's happening in the life of this person long ago. Very clearly, now, see what this young person is doing — and keep breathing . . .

Finally see your partner as a very old person. Where is this old person? What's happening? What does this old person look like? Does this old person have any words of wisdom to give you?

Before you begin to process this exercise, thank your partner. Now take a few minutes to talk together about the images you each saw. Tell each other what the images were before you begin to comment on them.

Next share how you felt doing the exercise. Did images come easily to you or did you have to struggle? Were you surprised by what you saw?

Now share how you responded to the images about yourself. Were they accurate for you or were they mainly your partner's projections? What did you learn about yourself?

This exercise is not everyone's cup of tea but I include it because there are many who have amazed themselves by it. They have felt clear contact without losing themselves. They have felt seen and recognized in a special, deep way. They have felt empathy and clairvoyance, personal power, pleasure, cooperation.

If this has been your experience, keep this feeling with you as you read the next chapter. We'll examine another level of moving beyond sexually isolating or fusing roles to sexual wholeness, and some specifics of healing sexual dysfunction.

❧ SEVEN ❧

Reclaiming
Sexual Pleasure

You were born with the capacity for sexual pleasure. But you may not have grown up with your pleasure capacity intact. Traumatic sex or skewed sexual messages may have thwarted it, at least to some extent, and tapping into it now may take work, contradictory as this sounds.

Let's begin with some specifics of what you can do if you are beset by one or more of the sexual problems we have outlined. Reclaiming sexual pleasure is easier if you know how.

Some of the dysfunctions have relatively straightforward solutions. These solutions have been tested over time, and they are part of standard sex therapy. Other dysfunctions require a more complex approach. There are no foolproof solutions to these dysfunctions. Sex therapists have not yet discovered answers that work for almost everybody. However, if you can open yourself to alternative ways of making love, you may discover individual answers for yourself and you may do more than reclaim your abilities for sexual pleasure. You may enhance them.

A word of caution before we plunge into dealing with sexual dysfunctions. Many of these dysfunctions involve sexual intercourse. We live in an age where millions of people are infected with the deadly AIDS virus — and one of the most efficient ways of transmitting this virus is through unprotected sexual intercourse. Please keep yourself safe by using common sense, condoms and spermicide containing Nonoxynol-9. We will discuss safe sex in more detail later.

Rediscovering Desire

If you think either you or your partner suffers from chronically low desire, there are a number of tacks you can take. These tacks depend on where your low desire originates — in the present or in the past. Let's begin with an example of low sexual desire that originates in the present.

Brenda And Walt: Changing The Pattern

Brenda and Walt come into my office complaining about Brenda's "frigidity." In telling their story, the couple divulges that Walt has a habit of sleeping in his socks and underwear.

"I do it to save laundry," explains Walt, who has been on his own since the age of 14.

> Brenda admits: It really turns me off. He comes to bed in his yukky stuff he's been wearing all day and then he tries to nuzzle up to me. It makes me feel like he doesn't care about me. If he had any sensitivity at all, he'd wear the nice pajamas I give him for his birthday. Or if he wanted to make love with me, he'd hop into bed with nothing on at all.

If you have a here-and-now problem of sexual desire like Brenda and Walt, what can you do?

1. **Deal intimately with one another.** Make your wishes known. And let them be known in a straightforward way, not in a roundabout manner that leaves your partner guessing.

As soon as Brenda summoned up the courage to tell Walt directly that what he was wearing to bed turned her off, they were both in a position to negotiate about what to do. Other couples may need to discuss issues like the timing of lovemaking, the setting, the method of contraception or safe-sex techniques.

2. **Spend time together away from everyday responsibilities,** even if it's only a few minutes. Make dates with one another. Try being seductive and silly *out* of bed. You may feel a bit foolish, but acting out of the ordinary may free up your body and emotions, making them more mobile.

3. **Ask for the kind of direct sexual stimulation you need.** And ask for as much stimulation as you need.
Blocked desire may actually be blocked frustration. That is, in order not to feel the frustration, women may short-circuit the desire for sex. This is especially true for women who, time and again, have had the stimulation stop just as they are about to spill over into orgasmic release.
If you don't know how to begin talking directly about sex, then remember our earlier discussion about communication. Remember also, the great sexual communicators are the interdependent, cooperative roles, **Top Banana, Magnetic Maggie, Earth Mother, Wonder Woman,** and **Gloria Mundi.**

4. **Above all, to get something started, try something** *new.* When Walt was perplexed about what, besides changing his nightwear, he might do to excite Brenda's sexual interest, I gave him the following assignment:
Spend an hour making love to Brenda. You can do anything you want. Just don't go above her ankles.

The following week Brenda reported:

I had no idea he had that kind of tenderness in him or that kind of humor! He ended up cradling my feet on his chest and telling

This Little Piggy stories to my big toes. I started to cry because it was like being comforted when I was a little girl. And then I began to feel so sexy. But you said we couldn't go above the ankles. So he just stroked my feet until I came to climax. And then we broke the rules and held each other all over. I've never felt turned on like that before.

When your problem is a current one like Walt's and Brenda's, common sense is usually your most successful sex therapist. But the seeds of low sexual desire are often planted years before your present relationship — during a childhood of abuse, trauma or misinformation.

When old problems are blocking your sexual feelings, it's necessary to add the following to the guidelines above:

5. **Do whatever you can to understand the nature of your trauma (and/or your partner's) and come to grips with it.** A recovery path is also one of the paths to recovering sexual desire because it frees you to experience a full range of feelings. It also teaches you to stay solidly in the present even if your partner is whirling around in feelings that have nothing to do with your present relationship.

6. **Learn to relax.** This may not be easy if your major line of defense is to hold on tight but it is relaxation that allows sexual feelings to register as desire. To practice relaxing you can meditate, listen to tapes, take classes. To practice relaxing with your partner, you can use the breathing techniques mentioned earlier.

7. **Exercise.** This arouses energy, including sexual energy. Exercise is active. It can help you change your passive **Sleeping Beauty** and **Shrinking Violet** to a more lusty **Top Banana** or **Magnetic Maggie**. Exercise can also *exorcise* — by keeping you in the present instead of spaced back into past co-dependent roles. When your partner is turned off sex, you can try exercising away pushy **Big**

Bertha, ever-pleasing Total Woman, and ever-needy Little Match Girl.

8. **Make friends with your inner child (or children)** — and also your partner's. You have already met your *waif* and your *elf.* They are a source of your basic emotions and they hold a key to your sexual desire now.

9. **Finally, remember you have a right to desire sex.** You also have a right to be desired. Remember too that important as your partner may be, you are the most important person in your life. If you feel desirable but your partner is not coming through for you, you can give yourself sexual pleasure and take some of the neediness out of your relationship.

Releasing Your Orgasms

Orgasm is an absolutely normal function for women. It has been documented in earliest infancy and in old age. Women have reported experiencing orgasm from genital stimulation and from nongenital stimulation. They've even reported orgasm from no physical stimulation at all — a Think-Orgasm, as one woman put it. Yet there's a fair percentage of women who have problems reaching orgasm or who have never come to orgasm their whole lives long. If you are one of these women, what do you do to release the orgasms that are part of your birthright?

The guidelines that follow are culled from the sex therapy literature and also from my clinical experience. If you're already orgasmic, some of these guidelines may lead you to even more pleasure with your orgasms. Like problems with desire, orgasmic dysfunction may be a result of present, common-sense difficulties or it may be deeply rooted in the past. Let's start with here-and-now solutions.

Guidelines For Orgasmic Function

1. **Make sure you have the right kind of stimulation.**

The answer to orgasm for you may be as simple as making sure you get enough of what you want. In the sexual dark ages, before Kinsey and Masters and Johnson, it was believed that the only right way for women to come to orgasm was through vaginal stimulation, by intercourse — with their husbands. The problem was that an estimated 80 percent of those women never came to orgasm.

Since the 1970s, researchers have learned much more about how women come to orgasm. First of all, it is acknowledged that not all women's partners are husbands and that not all sex is intercourse.

It is now well documented that many women can come to orgasm only if their clitorises are stimulated and only if they are stimulated in a special way for a certain amount of time. It is also documented that some women are most orgasmic by stimulation of their G Spots, an area about the size of a quarter in the front wall of the vagina.

Other women need all-over touching before they can come. Some women are not as turned on by vaginal stimulation and intercourse as they are by outercourse. Fondling, nuzzling or blowing on the neck, ears, toes or what have you, is more exciting to them than diving straight for the homing sites. Outercourse can be as important for heterosexual women as it is for lesbians.

Remember also that sex is more than physical. It is mental, spiritual and emotional as well. Along with physical stimulation, women may need fantasy to warm them up. And some women can come to orgasm only if they are in love or have romantic rituals or feel undying commitment from their mates.

Stimulation for orgasm is a highly individual matter. You may not be able to count entirely on a partner to figure this out for you, but you can find a great deal out for yourself by a technique urged by sex therapists the country over (also by piano teachers and basketball coaches): *Practice!*

Find some private time and space and try stimulating yourself until you find exactly the right combination of physical stimulation and fantasy. Try it in your bed or in your bathtub. Try it with your hand or with your shower nozzle. Vibrators can work like magic (but don't use them in your bathtub unless you want the fireworks to be more than sexual).

Once you've figured out your own favorite kinds of stimulation, you can share them with your partner. For additional information read *For Yourself* and *Sex for One*.

2. Practice Kegel exercises.

Developed by urologist Dr. Arnold Kegel to help patients control incontinence, these exercises involve toning up your pubycoccygeus muscle (PC muscle for short), the big muscle at the opening of your vagina that contracts when you come to orgasm.

If you tighten your PC muscle (as if you're stopping yourself from urinating) and then let it go (as if you're letting yourself urinate), you are actually mimicking the contractions of orgasm. Try tightening and letting go rhythmically — a few times at first and then up to 150 times a day. At the very least, it will help you get to know that your PC muscle exists. And at the most, you may find the exercises enjoyable, even to the point of orgasm. Mimicking orgasm may turn into the real thing.

3. Challenge your concept of normality.

Who says you've got to wear a T-shirt that says, *I finally reached The Big O?* And who says you have to arrive at your orgasms by a certain route? Line up your should-givers and have a look at them. You can write them down, draw pictures of them or represent them with pillows.

One client brought in photographs of her should-givers, spread them in a big circle around her on the floor and hopped back and forth between them until she decided she was just too tired to keep on hopping. She took control of the situation by gathering up the photos and stashing them back where they belonged — in her desk drawer.

Then she went to the bookstore and bought three books about women's orgasm: *The Hite Report, The G Spot* and *For Yourself.* She took a leave of absence from therapy to do some personal research and when she returned, it was to let me know that she no longer had problems with orgasm.

If one of your orgasm should-givers is your partner, this complicates matters. You can't just shut your partner in a desk drawer. You need to deal with him or her directly, calling on your most sexually assertive roles, like **Top Banana** and **Magnetic Maggie.**

This brings us to the point that releasing your orgasms is not always a matter of simple mechanics. Sometimes it involves your partner and sometimes it involves old feelings.

4. Flow with your partner's rhythms.

A flowing relationship is likely to encourage flowing sexual feelings. A flowing relationship also involves your taking the risk to get clear with your partner about what turns you on and off (of course you have to take the risk to get clear with yourself first). If what would help you relax into orgasm is rock music or a full-body massage, then allow yourself to ask for it. With a responsive partner, this becomes part of a mating dance you do together.

Hand Dance

To help you find your rhythm, try a hand dance together. Stand facing each other with your palms almost touching, as if you were about to give each other *high fives.* Then, in slow motion, one of you start moving your hands and the other follow, so that your palms are always almost touching. You can become quite lyrical as you follow each other's hands, passing leadership back and forth until it's impossible to know who's leading and who's following.

5. Let go of old feelings.

For some women, melting frozen rage or fear allows the rivers of orgasm to begin to run. When you hang on tight to traumatic scenes from the past you're storing old rage, terror and grief in your muscles, tensing them so that it becomes impossible to let go into orgasmic release. Try hanging tightly onto a pillow, scrunching every muscle to press it close and hunching over it so no one can see it. This degree of tension is exactly what's happening in bed when you're trying to come to orgasm.

Melting the tensions that prevent orgasm may require intensive therapy or at least intense support from those who love you, for it may be necessary for you to be in touch with feelings that were intolerable in the past. Feelings that made you want to murder, or dig a hole and die. I am in awe every time I walk another woman through such places of inner darkness, helping her scream, sob, pound, shake — until she begins to breathe fully again, able to let herself feel without fearing that she'll die or kill.

Whether you want to go this route to recover your capacity for orgasm is, of course, an individual choice. For some women, it's important to hold onto the rage and the other feelings. Whatever you decide, let the choice come from you and not from your partner or your therapist.

6. Examine your sexual co-dependencies.

- Are you a **Total Woman** who feels compelled to care for your partner and neglect your sexual self? Set aside a time period in each 24 hours just for you. The books say one hour a day, but if you know that would be self-defeating, how about starting with five minutes. Choose whatever period of time you can set aside and keep set aside.
- Do you think there must be something desperately wrong with you or your partner because you're not having orgasms on demand? Understanding more about how your orgasms work may help turn your blaming **Big Bertha** or self-blaming **Hostage Keeper** into playful, self-accepting **Wonder Woman**.

- Are you a sexually passive **Sleeping Beauty** or **Sponge?** Orgasm is a participatory sport. Learning how you can give yourself sexual pleasure or heighten the sexual pleasure with your partner can help you engage in the sexual scene. Taking charge of your own pleasure in this way can get you out from under the missionary position and turn you into a **Top Banana.**
- Do you believe sexual pleasure is somehow sinful or bad? This belief does not help you have the orgasms you want. Without getting into an argument about religious or moral matters, ask yourself if you want to be a **Match Girl**, victimized by the concept of sexual sin, or if you would rather activate your **Earth Mother,** who is both nurturing and self-nurturing.

7. Use your memories.

Follow your memory back to a time when you last came to orgasm. If you have never experienced orgasm, follow your memory to a time when you felt close to it. If you have never felt close to orgasm, follow your memory to before you turned off to any kind of good feelings.

Pleasant memories can revive feelings of pleasure and you can allow yourself to relive these feelings and update them to the present to help you flow into orgasmic release.

Celia: Recovering Memories

If you have no memories of orgasm, perhaps Celia's story will give you some ideas. Celia thought she had never had an orgasm, until she remembered her responses to hearing the church choir when she was six years old:

> I was awash with the music and the beauty of the people singing.
> I could feel my whole body moving and a warm sensation all
> through me. I must have been acting strange, because my mother
> slapped me on the side of my head and told me to hush up or she
> would have to take me home. I was so ashamed. I didn't know what

was happening to me, but I knew it must be something bad. Whenever I came close to that feeling again, I put it down fast.

Once Celia recovered the memory, she was able to re-establish the orgasm connection.

Letting Go Of Vaginismus

If your body is playing out its memories of physical, emotional or spiritual abuse by locking shut the door to your vagina, the therapy books say you have an excellent chance for a total cure. In just a few magic sessions you will be able to open up enough for successful intercourse. The standard sex therapy for vaginismus includes the following:

- Relaxation training. This may include working out the kind of imagery that encourages you to open up, such as visualizing your vagina as a flower changing from a tight bud to a full blossom. Relaxation sessions might also include hypnosis, with a post-hypnotic suggestion that your vaginal muscles will let go.
- Dilators gently inserted by a gynecologist, your partner, or yourself. These dilators are graduated, beginning with very narrow ones at first. They can be anything from surgical steel to your partner's fingers or your own. My personal preference is to suggest fingers over surgical steel because fingers are warm, alive and can convey loving feelings.

I regularly add to the standard sessions awareness exercises, such as the Kegel exercises outlined above, and full-body massage, to help you relax your whole body, not just your vaginal muscles. After all, it isn't just your vagina that's making love, it's all of you.

Most importantly, I encourage extensive exploration of the causes of the vaginismus. I also encourage couple therapy whenever it is relevant. There are two reasons for this. First it will acquaint your partner with all that you are going through — including reassessment of sexual goals for both of you.

Second it should gain sensitive support for you. I feel this work is crucial to long-term healing.

An effective way to work on the relationship fallout from vaginismus is to tend to your sexual co-dependencies.

- If you are a **Total Woman** or a **Ms. Goodbar** who gets your major satisfaction by pleasing a male partner, you may need to work on self-nurturing and assertiveness.
- If you are a **Shrinking Violet,** who needs to rely on his approval rather than work things out equally, then you may need to work on your self-esteem.
- If your only vision of normal is to be able to have "real" sex, i.e., intercourse, then you may need to expand your horizons to the thousand and one other ways you can give and receive sexual pleasure.

Precautions About Therapy

First, be warned about the "magic" treatment of vaginismus. While the symptom of vaginal spasm may quite quickly drop away under hypnotherapy and the relief may be joyous and real, the feelings surrounding the trauma that caused it are not necessarily healed — anymore than an alcoholic becomes sober the minute he or she gives up drinking.

Unless you deal in depth with the root causes of your vaginismus, another symptom may pop up to affect some other function of your life and this symptom could be worse than vaginal spasms.

Second, you may have vaginismus but it may not be a problem for you. In general, vaginismus does not affect your capacity for desire or for orgasm. If vaginal penetration is not how you want to make love, you don't have to let yourself be talked into "taking the cure" by a male partner who wants intercourse or by a doctor who assumes you want "normal" sex.

You can let them know that there are many ways to make vibrant, satisfying love and that your choice is something other than intercourse. Perhaps it's outercourse.

Healing Genital Pain

The first step in healing genital pain is to find out what the pain is, and that may mean finding good medical advice and supervision.

Infection Or Disease

Your problem may be due to infection or disease. Most infections or diseases don't just go away unless you do something to get rid of them. Ask your doctor to talk frankly with you about what's going on — not only about the treatment but about its affect on your sexuality. Also, if your partner needs to be treated too, ask your doctor to explain the treatment process to both of you as clearly and sex-positively as possible.

You may opt for treatment approaches that depart from traditional medicine. Homeopathic and herbal remedies can offer effective relief for some genital infections but they, too, are best administered with the advice of a professional.

Aside from medical intervention, there are probably steps you can take to take care of yourself and feel better. The steps can be as basic as changing your diet, taking baking-soda sitz baths or wearing skirts instead of tight pants to cut down on genital friction. A self-help book that is both informative and nonblaming is the *New Our Bodies, Our Selves*. Invoke your **Earth Mother** to help you take good care of yourself.

Injury

If your pain is due to injury or surgical injury, get at least two opinions on what can be done to rectify matters. If you determine that it's pain you've got to live with, find ways to make love that don't exacerbate the pain. In other words, change from intercourse to outercourse — and even say No to sex if need be. If your partner can't or won't understand, seek help for both of you from an accredited sex therapist.

Lack Of Lubrication

If your genital pain is due to lack of lubrication, then it is necessary to look at why you lack lubrication. If you are postmenopausal, lack of vaginal lubrication is part of the natural aging process. Otherwise lack of lubrication may be a problem in the excitement phase of your sexual response. Are you turned off by something your partner is doing — or not doing? Might you be turned on by something different? Read the section above on rediscovering desire. Especially important, allow yourself to masturbate using stimulation that is most likely to turn you on. You may find yourself lubricating when you can control the stimulation yourself. Let pleasure-loving **Gloria Mundi** be your guide.

If you do not produce enough lubrication for your comfort and pleasure, use another lubricant, such as K-Y Jelly. Do not use an oil-based lubricant such as Vaseline — it will block what natural lubrication you do have and it will disintegrate latex condoms on contact.

Abuse

If your genital pain is due to abuse, put a stop to the abuse immediately. You deserve to have sexual pleasure, not sexual pain. Sex is about cooperation and trust, not power tripping and objectification. Call on **Wonder Woman** and **Top Banana** to be your allies.

If it is not possible for you to stop the abuse or walk away from it, find help that will make it possible. There are battered women's support groups in many communities — women in these groups will understand what you are going through.

If your genital pain is due to body memories, the behavioral therapy outlined for vaginismus might help exorcise them. The same precautions apply, too.

Table 7.1. Detaching From His Dysfunction

Cooperative Detachment	Devastating Detachment
Let's bring me to orgasm before we have intercourse this time. I get so frustrated when you come first and then I feel left hanging	Oh, God, here we go again. I'm starting to get turned on and I know what's going to happen. You'll let me down again just as I'm about to explode. I just can't stand what a wimp you are in bed. I'm going to sleep on the sofa.
How about trying sex without intercourse tonight. I've always wanted to see if I can come without you inside me.	If you can't do any better than usual tonight, I don't know what I'm going to do. I might as well be living on my own for all the fun I get out of sex with you.
I'd like to do something this weekend besides make love. I can see how upset you get and I get upset, too. Perhaps instead we can talk about what's going on and figure out what to do or decide on looking for some outside help.	If you think I'm going to get in bed with you this weekend you've got rocks in your head. You're not even a man. If you don't go to a doctor and get fixed, I'm leaving.

Dealing With *His* Sexual Dysfunctions

Talk to most women whose partners have problems getting erections or coming too soon and they'll tell you:

It can make you crazy. Not only don't you get your own needs met, you're constantly trying to stroke his ego because he feels like half a man.

So your first task in dealing with a male partner's sexual dysfunction may be to detach and to remember the three C's — you didn't cause it, you can't control it and you can't cure it. It belongs to him. Even if you've been nasty to him or even if he admits his sexual dysfunction is to get back at you for something, it's still *his* sexual response. Of course it affects you, perhaps to the point of distraction, but if the dysfunction is going to change, he will have to change it, not you.

But how do I detach when I need him so much? After all, he's my husband. I can't just go out and get it from somebody else.

This is a common complaint I hear in my office.

Detachment can further communication or it can be devastating. Table 7.1 contains examples of both kinds, so you can see the difference.

If your partner comes too soon or has problems with erections, try saying each of the phrases in Table 7.1 out loud and see which ones might best further the kind of communication you want.

But no matter how successfully you attempt to detach from his sexual dysfunction, Masters and Johnson point out that there's no such thing as an uninvolved partner. Standard therapy techniques for both premature ejaculation and impotence inevitably include you. Not only for your information and support, but sometimes actually to help teach your partner skills.

Here are some specific therapy techniques for dealing with these dysfunctions.

Table 7.2. Sexual Recovery Self-Assessment Guide

Your Or Your Partner's Dysfunction	Your Need (Security, Self-Image, Nurturing, Power/Control Pleasure	Your Coopera-tive Styles (Top Banana, Magnetic Maggie, Earth Mother, Wonder Woman, Gloria Mundi)	Your Choices Of Recovery Techniques (Self-Awareness, Communication, Detaching, Peer groups, therapy)
Low Desire			
Anorgasmia			
Genital Pain Or Vaginisimus			
Premature Ejaculation			
Impotence			
Inhibited Initiation			
Whole-Person Disconnection			
Wanting Too Much			
Other			

Rx For Premature Ejaculation

Though his therapy may involve you, that doesn't mean you have to get hooked into doing all the work. It does mean that your focus and your support can be crucial in your partner's ability to do his work. Think about it. If the shoe were on the other foot, you'd want his help, too. But unless you were playing a passive, co-dependent role like **Sponge**, you wouldn't want him to run the show.

Any competent sex therapist can help guide you through the therapy for premature ejaculation. Or, if you want to try being your own sex therapist, you can read a detailed version of the steps in *The New Sex Therapy. Male Sexuality* also has some extremely helpful suggestions.

My office technique routinely goes like this: I explain that the problem is most probably that the man has lost contact with his penis somewhere along the line and that the task is for the two of them to get better acquainted. Clients may giggle at first but they usually get the point, fast.

Depending on the situation, we may then proceed with family history taking, sex education, couple therapy, grief and anger work, inner-child work. Eventually I'll suggest conversations with his penis. We will examine his sexual co-dependencies or at least probe to see if he has any.

Along with this emotional work, I give as homework the following standard behavioral steps for delaying ejaculation — and deal openly with any couples issues that arise along the way:

1. **The Stop-Start Technique:** The assignment is for him to masturbate at least once a day and to stop the minute he feels like coming to ejaculation. When the feeling subsides, he is to start again and stop again. And so forth. This will go on each day, for a week or two or more — until he has a sense of being able to control his ejaculation. At the end of each session he rewards himself by allowing himself to ejaculate.

This is important. Stop-Start is not a punishment, it's an adventure in consciousness-raising.

2. **The Squeeze Technique:** He may find it helpful to squeeze the glans of his penis each time he stops. Some men do and some don't. It's entirely a matter of what works.

3. **Partner Involvement:** When he has a good deal of control and sense of his own point of ejaculatory inevitability (isn't that a grand phrase? It has the ring of ancient Greek drama to me), that's where you come in. Sexual interdependence in this sense means that you cooperate with him in another few series of Stop-Starts and perhaps Squeezes. Each series should go on for about a week or more — until he has developed control over his ejaculation at each phase. And of course he gets rewarded at the end of each session by being allowed to ejaculate — and *you* get rewarded by being allowed to come to satisfaction any way you want.

The series goes like this:

• You masturbate him with your hand, stopping and squeezing when he tells you to.
• You masturbate him with your *lubricated* hand, stopping (and squeezing) when he tells you to.
• He lies on his back, you straddle his pelvis and guide his penis into your vagina. You control the thrusting, starting and stopping when he tells you to.

Using these exercises, eventually, he should be able to gain more or less complete control of his ejaculatory reflex.

Rx For Erectile Problems

Erectile problems can be much more difficult to bring under conscious control than coming too soon.

In the first place, possible organic causes need to be monitored by a physician. Erectile problems can be caused by dis-

ease, including diabetes, and medication, such as those pre-
scribed for high blood pressure. Substance abuse, smoking,
depression, stress, performance anxiety and sexual co-dependency issues — all these can cause or exacerbate erectile dysfunction. *The New Sex Therapy* contains a comprehensive list.

Current thinking is that a man is organically impaired if
he is unable to get erections during sleep. He will then have
to "learn to live with it" — which may mean learning new
and creative ways to make love with you. Or he may opt to
go the surgical route and have a penile implant. Yes, there is
such a thing if it makes a difference to you. You can obtain
information about it from your medical doctor or a certified
sex therapist.

Men can conduct their own preliminary sleep-lab experi-
ment at home to find out if they're physiologically able to have
erections. It's this simple: He pastes part of a roll of postage
stamps around his flaccid penis when he goes to bed. If the
stamps are torn when he wakes up, he's had an erection.

Whether he's able to have erections or not, he may benefit
from sex therapy. Sex therapy approaches vary widely. I tend
to stress a combination of relaxation techniques with intensive
psychotherapy, especially focusing on power issues —
including childhood abuse. Walking back down the power
road may be long and painful. And it's here that the key to
updating sexual potency often lies.

Couple therapy may become crucial here, not only to facilitate *his* recovery but to help keep you from going off the
deep end while he works it all through. After all, erection is
basically a response of the parasympathetic nervous system.
That is, no matter how hard he tries or how much stimulation
you give him, he cannot will his blood vessels to dilate and
make his penis hard and erect. What will ultimately make this
possible is his ability to let go into total relaxation — physical,
mental, emotional, spiritual.

This means that the more upset you become over his limp
penis, the harder he may have to work to recover his potency
— his power — especially if he's a co-dependent caretaker
who'd rather fix you than fix himself.

Help Him By Helping You

If your male partner has problems with erections or with coming too soon, you can be most helpful by taking care of yourself so that you don't become desperate with frustration and blow the whole relationship out of the water.

You can work on your own self-esteem, an essential part of your recovery. And you can learn options other than intercourse — options from massages to sensuous food-play. If you need how-to details, see *Safe Encounters*.

In addition, you can examine your own co-dependency issues:

- You can burst the great American myth that says men are all powerful by substituting the message that you are powerful too. Not with the power of blame or self-blame but with **Wonder Woman** magic — the kind of power that wants to play and wants to share.
- You can transform your **Total Woman** to **Earth Mother**. Instead of compulsively giving to him, in an effort to make him a "real" man, you can learn how to ask for satisfaction from him.
- Perhaps most important, you can learn not to depend on his undependable penis. Learn to satisfy yourself. Depend on you first.

Taking care of Number One puts you in an emotional position where it is possible to have a sexually cooperative attitude. Instead of blaming him or trying to fix him, make sure you do the following:

1. Talk openly about what's going on. Don't try to rescue his ego by keeping your feelings to yourself.
2. Ask for what you want.
3. Treat him with respect. Even if he's got sexual problems, he's still a human being and you've chosen him as your partner.

Learning To Initiate

It's not that you don't want sex. It's that you can't get yourself to ask for it. The *Don't Ask* dysfunction goes to the roots of every woman's tendencies for sexual co-dependency. To post-traumatic stress, where the teaching is Don't Talk; to cultural messages that say, "Men Are in Control, Don't Worry Your Pretty Head About a Thing;" to the developmental psychosexual brainwashing that Nice Girls Don't.

Sleeping Beauty, who lies under glass waiting to be discovered, is a prime example of inhibited initiation. But you don't have to wait around for Prince or Princess Charming while the brambles grow up around you. This is nearly the 21st century. You can call on any of your cooperative roles to help you become a sexual activist in your own right! If you need to justify yourself with a motive other than your own pleasure, know that being able to initiate sex and ask for the kind of sex you want puts you in a much safer and saner position, especially in this age of AIDS.

The communication problem that results in the inability to initiate sex stems from three gaps you can usually do something about: information, self-esteem and practice.

Information

You can use chapter 5 as a guide to the kinds of sexual information you need. If you read it carefully and do the exercises (I mean really do them), you will learn much about your psychosexual upbringing and about your view of what sexually normal is.

In addition, there are books listed in the bibliography that deal explicitly with every possible sexual subject: women's sexual response, men's sexual response, masturbation, fantasy, lesbian and gay lifestyles, safe sex, sex therapy, rape, incest and child sexual abuse. These will not only provide a smorgasbord for thought, they'll offer you the comfort that other people besides you have thought about these issues.

Self-Esteem

Your recovery is essential to rebuilding your sense of sexual self. For many women I see in therapy, their self-esteem was shattered so early, they feel they have to start rebuilding from ground zero.

Contradictory as it sounds, self-esteem doesn't originate from inside. Developmentally, it starts from the outside, when you are a baby, with loving feedback that validates your inner sense of well-being. So even if you're a control freak who's got to Do It All Yourself, you may need some help rebuilding sexual self-esteem. At the very least, you're likely to need the validation of books, your peer group, your therapist. If you have supportive family and friends and a partner who cares about your sexual recovery, your feedback system will be a solid one.

However, you can't rely totally on others for your self-esteem. Jennifer, the client you've met in previous chapters, admitted early on in her therapy:

> I feel like a leaky bucket. As fast as Martin pours in love and praise, it runs out again.

How do you plug the hole in the bottom of your self-esteem bucket? This task is individual for every woman. Jennifer did it over a period of time by a series of disciplined approaches.

First, she came to understand her seemingly inevitable vulnerability. After a while, she was able to know ahead of time what kinds of sexual situations were going to plunge her back into feeling like a victim. This knowledge allowed her to exercise the choices she had:

- To remove herself from the situation.
- To change the situation.
- To ride out the old feelings.

As she became clearer about her choices, she became clearer about her own self-worth. She began to make moves to enhance it. For instance, she joined a choral group. The singing opened her chest, helped strengthen her voice and gave her a sense of natural cooperation as she learned to make music along *with* the group, without having to either lead or follow.

Practice

This means taking the risk of trying out new behaviors and it means trying things out more than once, until you get the knack. True, you probably never got nearly as much chance for sexual rehearsal play when you were growing up as the boys did (after all, Nice Girls *Don't*). But you can do something about this now — unless you want to be known as a Nice Girl into your golden years.

When Enough Is Not Too Much: Options To Sexual Obsession And Addiction

Kicking a sexual habit that's out of control is not the same as kicking drugs or alcohol. You can't Just Say No to sex, put it behind you and expect to begin successfully to pick up the other pieces of your life. Nor can you responsibly teach your children: Stay away from sex, it'll just make you nuts or kill you.

Recovering from sexual obsession and addiction is more like recovering from out-of-control relationships with food or work, for like food and work, sex is integral to your life. Your feelings and responses to sex are connected to your feelings and responses to everything else, even if it's been your defensive pattern to try to keep them separate.

Sexual recovery means coming to terms with your whole sexual self so that you can make your sexual thoughts and actions work for you, not against you.

All of the exercises in this book are potentially helpful for sexual obsession and addiction:

- Understanding your old sexual scripts and family messages are vital awareness-raisers.
- Learning to ask directly and positively for what you want can help keep you from slipping into old, self-compromising communication patterns.

- Discussion about specific dysfunctions may help fill important gaps in your understanding of how your sexual response functions.

Above all, the road from addiction to satisfaction involves a change in how you think and feel about your sexual relationships, and about how you approach them. Recovery involves a role shift from co-dependency to wholeness.

Forever Amber and Shrinking Violet, forever scared, can become Top Banana, in charge and able to negotiate the kinds of relationships that offer the security she wants and needs.

Total Woman, so pleasing — and so sad, becomes Magnetic Maggie, who attracts partners who are responsive to her and give her the positive feedback she wants and needs.

Enabling Ms. Goodbar and needy Match Girl become generous but self-nurturing Earth Mother. When her partner can't take care of her, she can take care of herself.

Ever-demanding Big Bertha and ever-entrapping Hostage Keeper become Wonder Woman, whose approach is playful magic rather than a heavy hand. This gives her a feeling of inner power and control that does not require manipulating her partner.

Hit-and-run artist Mata Hari and never-filled Sponge become Gloria Mundi, who revels in the pleasure and satisfaction that come from sexual intimacy.

What About Abstinence?

A period of abstinence may help — not so much to "cure" your habit as to find out what happens when you stop. You may find you're using certain sexual patterns to substitute for feelings you weren't able to cope with when you were younger, such as grief or anger or failure. If you remove these patterns for a time, your old feelings will have a chance to make themselves known to you. You may not be happy to acknowledge them but at least you'll begin to get a handle on what your sexual excesses are all about. Remember the old saying: The truth will make you free — but first it will make you miserable.

Note that by suggesting a period of abstinence I'm not in any way suggesting that sex is bad. A negative attitude about sex will not help you move from sexual obsession and addiction to the ability to make choices for healthy, pleasurable sex. Be wary of programs that are based primarily on abstinence or that give you the message that sex is a disease or that sexual pleasure is morally wrong.

For long-term healing, it's essential that you deal directly with any sexual problems somewhere along the line. To do this you need to find a course of therapy or a peer group that offers you the following:

1. A sex-positive attitude
2. Sex education
3. Support for yourself as a sexual being.

Although recovery from sexual obsession and addiction is significantly different from recovering from alcohol and drug abuse, there are also some strong parallels:

• Both sex and drugs produce a chemical high and there are withdrawal symptoms when you change behaviors.
• Both addictions may be compounded by relationship co-dependencies.
• Both addictions are often viewed as signs of sinfulness or immorality.
• Both addictions are often viewed as signs of weak will-power.
• A positive parallel is that there are now support groups all over the country for dealing with addictions of all sorts — even sex.

The Cycle Of Sexual Satisfaction: Reversing The Popcorn-Bowl Syndrome

When you no longer need to use sex as part of a disappearing act from situations and feelings that are intolerable, sexual satisfaction begins to replace obsession and addiction.

Here we have the opposite of the Popcorn-Bowl mechanics

described earlier, with the never-ending cycle of existential split, unaware reaching and wanting too much.

Existential Integration: You have made yourself aware of connections between your past and present and are able to acknowledge and accept your formerly intolerable feelings. You have opened connections between your mind, body, soul and emotions. You understand how sexuality affects the rest of your life and how the rest of your life affects sex.

When you reach out for sexual stimulation, you reach out with your whole being. You know you have more than one choice of stimulation open to you. You believe you are going to be satisfied.

Positive Sexual Choices: You choose partners and kinds of stimulation that most effectively please and satisfy.

Experiencing Enough: No matter what the exact stimulation, you are aware of your own rhythms and you are sensitive to your partner's rhythms. You can relax in the knowledge that this is not the last sex you'll ever have in your life; you can have more when you want it in the future. This knowledge helps you thoroughly enjoy what's there today.

Diagrammed, the cycle of sexual satisfaction looks like Figure 7.1:

10 Signs Of Recovery From Sexual Obsession And Addiction

1. You are conscious of how sex creates intimacy between you and your partner.
2. You enjoy sex with a partner, and although you may need it for emotional and physical release you don't feel as if you're going to die if you don't get it. Besides, you can take care of your own sexual needs.
3. You know what enough feels like.
4. You are generally happy with the ways you make love, and you have enough flexibility to know there's more than one route to sexual satisfaction.
5. You repeat sexual scenarios that enhance your sexual pleasure and lead to emotional closeness.

6. You enjoy thinking about sex, but you can choose to think about other aspects of life that are important to you, too.

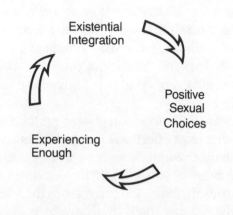

Figure 7.1. The Cycle Of Sexual Satisfaction.

7. You understand and respect the difference between appropriate sexual relationships and relationships where sexual advances are inappropriate — for instance with your co-workers or with your children.
8. You understand the differences between safe relationships and unsafe ones — and you put relationship safety and well-being ahead of your need for sex.
9. You make sexual decisions that promote health, welfare, and joy in your life as a whole.
10. You make sexual decisions that take into account the well-being of your significant others, including your children.

Let's return to the stories of Barbara, who described herself as an addict, and Jennifer, who described herself as obsessive.

Barbara 4: Beyond Addiction

Barbara is the self-diagnosed Bad Girl who decided to swear off sex cold turkey because it was landing her in so much trouble. Almost immediately, she became painfully sick with arthritis. We left her feeling thoroughly discouraged and victimized, with no clear direction for recovery.

After I got sick enough, I finally made the connection that it wasn't sex that was my problem. It was me. Or rather it was that I had fragmented myself so much, I was flying off in all directions.

Until I stopped running, my pain took all sorts of forms. First it was all those one-night stands that finally made me feel like a dirty old lady. Then it was my joints swelling so that I couldn't walk.

What I had to deal with was my own neediness, that deprived little girl who lived inside me who wanted me to stop and hug her. Once I started spending some time with her I found out she'd let me know how to take care of her. Simple things like going to bed early so I wouldn't be tired the next day. And in learning to take care of her, I learned to take care of me.

Also I had to develop some new social skills. All my contact had come from sex. I didn't know how to say, "Hello." I only knew how to say, "Let's go to bed." So part of getting well for me was learning how to make small talk. That was hard because I had to start listening to what other people were saying so I could respond to them. And then I found that other people were listening to me, too. I think I bottomed out when I realized that I had lived all these years without ever having been heard. The grief was astounding. And when I finally stopped crying enough to look around, the joy was astounding.

After all this soul-searching, I rediscovered that I'm a passionate person. Passionate because I love pleasure, not because I'll die if I don't get the sex. Part of taking care of myself is validating that passion is okay and that sex is okay.

They say when you're ready the right person will appear to you. Well, I've been blessed with a new lover who is in recovery too and who is tender and responsive to me. It's really scary but we're taking it a day at a time. And we're daring to tell each other what we like and what we don't like. Even though it's scary, it's almost easy. Like that's the way it was supposed to have been all along.

Jennifer 4: Freedom From Obsession

To illustrate recovery from sexual obsession, let's hear from Jennifer again — obsessed with intercourse and married to Martin, who is impotent. We left her struggling through depression and gaining self-esteem.

> I joined a Sexaholics Anonymous group but the people in it weren't really interested in dealing positively with sex. They helped me be not so depressed and immobilized but not how to have sex with Martin.
>
> So I started reading everything I could about sex and I found a different group and a therapist who would keep me on track and work with us as a couple. It was up and down and it took a long time but little by little I learned that I had options besides taking to my bed and sulking when he couldn't get an erection.
>
> The most important thing I learned was that I could take care of myself — with my vibrator. This gave me all sorts of confidence. My obsessing about intercourse just sort of drifted away. I think about other things now. I joined a choir. I've got a part-time job. I'm writing poetry again.
>
> And Martin and I have a wonderful time in bed together. We may not have sex the way we used to because he still doesn't get erections very often. But it feels much better. We relate to each other in bed. Now I have love even if I don't have intercourse.

Whole-Person Sexual Connection: The Art Of Feeling Good

Whole-person sexual connection means that your sexual responses flow positively through body and soul, mind and emotions. It is the embodiment of sexual interdependence and it involves the playing out of any and all of your sexually cooperative roles, from **Top Banana** to **Gloria Mundi**.

Whole-person connection is characterized by the emotional and spiritual components of sex. These are so often overlooked in this goal-oriented, hurry-up society. Overlooked, too, in the scientific laboratory, where it's easier to document durations and frequencies than perceptions and feelings.

The characteristics of whole-person sexual connection are:
- Playfulness and romance
- Love
- Commitment
- Nurturing
- Intimacy
- *JOY.*

All of these characteristics are unmeasurable. Yet they are the aspects of sex that women have told me are most often the essential ingredients in their peak sexual experiences. They are especially poignant for recovering women, for they all mean that women have developed the ability to feel — with full power and memory.

Every woman's route to whole-person sexual connection is individual. This book is filled with pieces of women's journeys to wholeness. Let's hear again from Julia, whose husband forced sex on her and whose co-dependent response had been to numb out — and overnurture Carl. When we met her earlier, her rage was burning out of control.

Julia 3: A Sense Of Wholeness

I finally got incredibly ill. I even lost my voice and couldn't speak. What a punishment for being so angry! I just had to lie there and let Carl take care of me and the baby. There wasn't a blessed thing else I could do.

And you know what happened? He did take care of us. This is a man who'd never had to think about anybody but himself in his whole life. He took sick leave from work and he nursed us. He fed bottles to the baby and made meals. He changed diapers. He even washed me. He did all these things without questioning and without my having to do something to earn them.

At first I was so sick I thought he was an angel. Honestly, I thought I'd died and gone to heaven. Then when I began to get a little better, I got terrified again. Terrified of what? That it would stop? That I'd have to become more deserving? That I'd have to have sex with him? I didn't know. And then I began to remember those times my uncle made me pull down my pants and got in bed with me. I mean really remember them. They were when I was sick and he'd be the only one home.

The more I remembered, the more Carl just held me and rocked me. For days, it seemed, until I couldn't cry any more. I don't know how long it went on. All I know is that when it was over, I looked at this man who was my husband and the father of my child and for the first time I could see all the way through his eyes into his mind and his soul. And I just let him hold me while my whole body let go. It was beyond orgasm. It was beyond sex. There was a sense of wholeness and bonding and eternity.

For Julia, as for so many women who have confided their stories to me, the beginning of whole-person connection feels like magic. Like looking into the ruins of a bombed-out building and suddenly finding a proud and brilliant flower growing up out of the rubble.

Such a moment can be utterly liberating for some women but it can be utterly terrifying for others. Why? Because joy means opening up. It means letting go of control. It means having to remember life before the incest or the rape or the drinking or the messed-up childbirth. It means having to confront the terrible pain of the loss of innocence. And joy may mean giving up the fantasy that things are ever again going to be the way they were before you were violated, or the way you wished they might have been.

When you can open up, let go, remember, confront and give up — all to allow joy into your life — you are mistress of the art of feeling good.

Sexual Recovery: A Self-Assessment Guide

You can use this assessment guide to help you organize your thoughts about your sexual recovery.

- What cooperative roles will help you counter the sexual problems you have?
- What techniques can you use to detox your sex life and help you feel sexual pleasure?

This guide outlines the common sexual dysfunctions and relates them to possible solutions, such as cooperative roles and recovery techniques. To make your own assessment, complete Table 7.2, adding any categories of your own to tailor it to your situation.

Table 7.3. Sexual Recovery Self-Assessment Guide

Your Or Your Partner's Dysfunction	Your Need (Security, Self-Image, Nurturing, Power/Control Pleasure)	Your Cooperative Styles (Top Banana, Magnetic Maggie, Earth Mother, Wonder Woman, Gloria Mundi)	Your Choices Of Recovery Techniques (Self-Awareness, Communication, Detaching, Peer groups, Therapy)
Low Desire			
Anorgasmia			
Genital Pain Or Vaginisimus			
Premature Ejaculation			
Impotence			
Inhibited Initiation			
Whole-Person Disconnection			
Wanting Too Much			
Other			

❈ EIGHT ❈

From Toxic Sex To Safe Sex — Preventing AIDS And Other Physical Dangers

Safety is a crucial condition for satisfying, life-enhancing sex. The previous chapters have outlined many of the conditions you need for emotional sexual safety and have offered a number of options for detoxing sexual situations.

What about physical dangers? These can include an unwanted pregnancy or the deadly disease of AIDS or the ravages of other sexually transmitted diseases (STDs). Herpes, chlamydia, trichomonas, genital warts, some yeast infections (candida albicans), along with the classic "venereal diseases" (gonorrhea and syphilis), are all considered to be STDs. In this age where sex is posing more and more dangers to women, is physical sexual safety possible?

Yes. It is possible not only to have sex with relative safety but to have relatively safe sex with pleasure. This combination means taking charge of the physical aspects of your sexual safety, just as you have taken charge of the emotional aspects. The purpose of this chapter is to raise your safe-sex IQ. However, it is not to detail absolutely everything you need to know about preventing STDs or an unwanted pregnancy. An excellent guide for this already exists in the *New Our Bodies, Our Selves.*

An essential step in taking charge is to know what you're up against. What are the dangers? Let's start with pregnancy.

Unwanted Pregnancy

Pregnancy is a blissfully desired state for some women but it is far from that for others and there are conditions that make it downright dangerous. One of these conditions is disease. If you are infected with AIDS, for instance, pregnancy will intensify your symptoms, and there's a better than 50 percent chance you'll pass the virus along to your baby. A pregnancy can also be dangerous if you are unable to care for yourself or your baby — because you are too young, too poor, too traumatized. Pregnancy also is dangerous if the man you live with is violent.

If a woman wants to end her dangerous pregnancy, the issue of abortion presents yet another danger. When I was growing up, it was common to hear of coat-hanger abortions and of women bleeding to death on kitchen tables. In the early Seventies it became legal for women to have medically safe abortions. The right to safe abortion is being systematically challenged now by a political administration that says women should not be allowed to choose to end a pregancy. At this writing, there are already several states in which a woman cannot obtain a safe abortion unless she has the money and whatever other support she needs to travel across state lines.

Sexually Transmitted Diseases

What are the dangers presented by sexually transmitted diseases? AIDS is the only one of the STDs that is both fatal and has no cure, but all of them can threaten the quality of your life. The physical miseries of a chronic yeast or herpes infection can ruin sexual desire. Furthermore, they can affect a baby during the birth process. Untreated chlamydia or genital warts can lead to sterility or cervical cancer.

Beyond the physical difficulties, you can poison yourself with anger at the partner who transmitted the disease — especially if the partner knew he was infected and didn't tell you. You can immobilize yourself with guilt for having entered into the relationship. You can withdraw from sex entirely out of fear of passing STDs along. Taboos about mentioning sexual diseases may leave you with no one to talk to. And to compound your problems, your doctor may be judgmental or not fully informed.

Sexual Co-dependency And Unsafe Sex

Sexual co-dependency can make you a prime candidate for unsafe sex. Extreme neediness, low self-worth, lack of self-awareness, little practice in taking care of yourself — all these can lead directly to sexual behaviors that lead to disease and unwanted pregnancy.

It's crucial to underscore here, however, that it's not co-dependency that causes pregnancy or transmits AIDS and other STDs. You get pregnant from unprotected vaginal intercourse. You contract STDs from specific sexual behaviors with an infected partner. The riskiest of these behaviors is unprotected intercourse, either vaginal or anal, because it is intercourse that most efficiently allows the exchange of semen and blood, the fluid environments that are most compatible to the AIDS virus.

Suppose you've worked long and hard at being **Wonder Woman** or **Earth Mother**. Suppose you do everything right and still get pregnant or end up with a case of herpes? Suppose you do everything right and contract the AIDS virus? It can happen. Mistakes can occur. Condoms can break. This is not to terrify you into never having sex again, but to urge you to be kind to yourself no matter what happens. You don't have to add self-blame to your problems and you don't have to take blame from anyone else.

Although sexual wholeness is no guarantee of physical safety, co-dependent sexual behaviors are more likely to lead to problems. The following are particularly susceptible to risky sexual encounters:

- **Forever Amber,** who can't say No
- **Sleeping Beauty,** who is virtually unconscious during sexual encounters
- **Shrinking Violet,** who feels she has no rights
- **Total Woman** and **Ms. Goodbar,** who would die rather than offend
- **Mata Hari,** who'll sleep with anybody just for the sport
- **Poor Little Match Girl,** who'll do anything to keep a partner from leaving her
- **Sponge,** who accepts crumbs — and who takes Crumbs as lovers.

You are in a much better position for sexual encounters that are safe if your sexual approach is interdependent rather than co-dependent. **Top Banana, Magnetic Maggie, Earth Mother, Wonder Woman** and **Gloria Mundi** combine responsibility with their search for pleasure. They value themselves enough to know what they want, ask for what they want, choose safe relationships and practice only those sexual behaviors that are physically safe as well as emotionally and spiritually safe.

Let's look at exactly what you can do to keep yourself free of AIDS and other STDs.

Safe Sex In Theory And Practice

Because it's not okay in this culture to talk frankly and positively about sex, much of our safe-sex education is generalized, negative and quite impractical. Unless you belong to the gay community, seek out a special support group or otherwise go out of your way to learn about safe sex, your education is likely to be limited to watching TV commercials, reading newspapers or sitting opposite a poster on a bus. Mostly, safe-sex advice is the same kind of advice women have heard for years about how to avoid unwanted pregnancy:

- Just Say No.
- Be monogamous.
- Use condoms.

While this advice is sound in theory, it doesn't go far enough and it's not entirely practical for women. Moreover, if the advice doesn't work, it can leave women feeling guilty, as if they've caused bad things to happen to them.

Let's look at these guidelines one by one:

. . . Just Say No (Abstinence)

In the first place, most women don't know how to say No to sexual intercourse in a way that deters the men who are determined to have intercourse with them. This is especially true if you're locked into co-dependent role-playing around your sexuality. But even if a woman is crystal clear, just saying No is not enough to stop rape.

Also, No is not the whole answer for women's sexual safety. You cannot abstain from sex and expect the rest of your life to bloom with health. Besides, abstinence may backfire. It can create such feelings of deprivation that when critical mass is reached you may go for sex no matter what the consequences. As humorist Ogden Nash put it: "Abstinence makes the heart grow fonder."

According to AIDS educators, celibacy is different from total abstinence. It means not having sex with a partner — or at least not having genital sex with a partner. But safely celibate can certainly mean sexual. It can include masturbation, romance and nongenital touching — any activity that does not involve the exchange of body fluids.

Abstinence or celibacy may well be a safe haven at certain times in your life. For instance, you may need periods of backing off from sex to develop your own independence — a preliminary for moving close again, this time to cooperative wholeness. Or you may be a single mother or a career woman without the time or energy to develop sexual relationships. Or you may be concerned about AIDS.

But try talking abstinence or celibacy to a teenager whose hormones are popping or to a woman in love. In the long run, most women need to find a sex-positive approach that will help them develop satisfying, life-affirming sexual *partnerships.*

. . . Be Monogamous

This isn't the whole answer either.

If you think about it, to be really safe, monogamy means having only one partner your whole life long. This sets unrealistic standards for most women of today.

It presents potential dangers, too, ones that have nothing to do with AIDS. Lifelong monogamy has not necessarily been safe for women over the centuries. Unbreakable marriage contracts have virtually enslaved women, causing enormous fear, pain and deprivation. They provide the original models for sexual co-dependency, from **Forever Amber** to **Sponge.** Today's monogamous contracts may hold much more potential for sexual autonomy and interdependence, at least among Western women (after all, we've come a long way, baby) but unquestioning monogamy is still fertile ground for the culture of sexual co-dependency.

In terms of pregnancy, just because you have one lifelong partner doesn't necessarily mean that he is a safe partner for you or a safe father for your children. Horrifying statistics on marital rape and incest are coming more and more to light as researchers learn to ask women relevant questions.

In terms of AIDS, even if you live up to the monogamy standard, who's to say your partner will? Marital cheating is a sad fact of American life. It's estimated that more than 50 percent of couples are having affairs — and possibly bringing infections back home.

Finally, studies show that women's pattern of contracting AIDS is different from men's patterns — especially gay men, who tend to have multiple partners. Women are more likely to become infected through continuous contact with one infected partner. In other words, just because you're monogamous doesn't necessarily mean you're safe.

It's important to bring up the subject of sexual safety even if you have only one partner and even if you've been with him for a long time. If either of you has used IV drugs or had other sexual relationships in the last 10 years, you may be at risk of contracting the AIDS virus.

. . . Use Condoms

Again, advice for condom use is great in theory. Latex condoms, properly used — with a spermicide — can be an effective barrier for everything from the AIDS virus to unwanted sperm. What the media fails to mention is that condom use still presents a degree of risk. While condoms and spermicide can make intercourse *safer* in the age of AIDS, they do not make it entirely *safe*. Another problem is that most women do not know how to use condoms and are embarrassed to ask. Since the media doesn't discuss the specifics, women are left mystified about the basics of using condoms, spermicides and also latex gloves and dams, as well as other equipment that can help make sex safer.

Condoms may not be the whole answer for contraception either. Contraceptive technology also includes diaphragms, intrauterine devices (IUDs) and the Pill. IUDs and the Pill may be appealing because you don't have to bother with them during each sexual encounter, but they can cause serious health problems — from sterility to fatal blood clots. It is imperative that you make yourself aware of the pros and cons of the contraceptive possibilities so that you can choose what will work best for you.

If you don't have a doctor you feel you can talk to about these possibilities, search out a Planned Parenthood or women's clinic in your community.

Everywoman's Guide To Sexual Safety

Preventing unwanted pregnancy, or AIDS and other STDs is possible — and can be a positive aspect of your sexual relationship — if you stick to these three principles:

1. **Safe sex starts with your self-esteem.** If you value yourself you are likely to choose safe sexual situations and also take measures to make sure sex is as safe as it can possibly be.
2. **Safe sex means interdependent relationships not co-dependent ones.** Clarity, communication and care for self as well as others — these are The Three Cs for Safe Sex. They do not exist in co-dependent relationships.
3. **There's more to sex than intercourse.** Creativity is a fourth C that can enhance your sex life as well as help you stay free of sexual disease and unwanted pregnancy.

Let's put these principles in their most practical form, with a list of Do's and Don'ts. These are geared especially for women dealing with issues of sexual co-dependency and sexual cooperation. They are aimed primarily at women with male partners (or potential male partners) because AIDS and other STDs are primarily transmitted by the act of intercourse, while pregnancy is always a result of intercourse.

What follows is an outline only, to give you an idea of the issues. Please do not take these Do's and Don'ts as all you need to know about safe sex. All these ideas and many more are spelled out in great detail in *Safe Encounters.*

Safe Sex Don'ts

1. *Don't imagine it'll never happen to you.* Just because you're not informed doesn't mean you're immune to sexual consequences and dangers.

2. *Don't assume a potential partner is safe because he seems like a nice guy.* And don't be a Nice Girl who doesn't ask questions.

3. *Don't expect your partner to make all the preparations for safer sex.* He might not want to use condoms. He might forget the condoms some night. It is quite possible that he is not as concerned for your welfare as you are.

4. *Don't stick rigidly to the idea of intercourse as the only way to have sex.* You'll severely limit your safe-sex options, to say nothing of your pleasure!

5. *Don't say yes to sex just because you're feeling needy, or because you want to please him.* Shrinking Violet, Poor Little Match Girl or Ms. Goodbar can land you in trouble — or worse.

6. *Don't drink or drug before or during your sexual encounters.* This is as unsafe as mixing drinking or drugging with driving. Alcohol and drugs fog judgment, memory and boundaries, making it difficult for you to say No to unsafe sex or to cope with condoms during intercourse. Alcohol and drugs also depress the immune system, leaving you more susceptible to disease. Also, using needle drugs is a well-publicized route for the deadly AIDS virus.

7. *Don't believe that a negative AIDS test is proof that a potential partner is safe for you.* Testing is *not* a foolproof indicator of the AIDS virus. It indicates only whether antibodies have or have not developed in the blood in response to the virus. Since it can take six months to a year for these antibodies to develop, it is possible for people to show a negative test when they are in fact infected.

Safe Sex Do's

1. *Work on your sexual self-esteem.* Any of the exercises in this book may help. Be sure to call on Top Banana or any of your other whole-person roles. Self-worth is your first line of sexual defense.

2. *Choose a partner with great care.* Remember, in terms of physical infection, you're having sex with every sexual partner he has ever had. If he is a toxic person, you can be infected with more than a physical disease. You can be infected emotionally and spiritually, too.

- Interview him before you make the decision to go to bed with him. I know this sounds formal, and you'll have to use your good sense about just how tactful you want to be. At the very least, you want to find out how likely he is to be infected with the AIDS virus: Has he used IV drugs and shared needles? Has he had a blood transfusion in the last 10 years? Has he had sex with HIV-infected partners?

- **Do not have intercourse with him** if you have a reason to believe that he might be HIV-infected or infected with any other STD.
- **Check him out for symptoms** even if he leads you to believe he's free of infection. You can find STD symptoms listed in the *New Our Bodies, Our Selves,* but be aware that the AIDS virus doesn't have obvious symptoms. People can be infected without knowing it. Let him know that the only sex you'll have is safe or safer sex — sex with condoms and spermicide. Find ways to let him know that safe sex or safer sex can be fun for both of you.
- **Be immovable that it is safe or nothing,** even if he tries to sweet-talk you into "natural" sex "just this once." If he's not interested in your sexual safety, he's not interested in *you.* Do not agree to go to bed with him.
- **If he starts to get pushy or violent,** use any means to get as far away from him as you can. Call for help if at all possible.

3. *Be prepared.* If you do decide to have intercourse, make sure it doesn't take you by surprise. Your **Earth Mother** can help you take care of the mechanics — and also provide the sensitivity necessary to carry off the mechanics with grace, good humor and sensuality.

- **Keep condoms at the ready.** Using condoms can prevent all sexually transmitted diseases as well as an unwanted pregnancy.

    Condoms are not foolproof, but used correctly they can decrease the likelihood of unwanted consequences.

    You can choose a variety of kinds to suit your mood. Be sure they're latex, not lambskin (lambskin may let the miniscule AIDS virus through — it's smaller than

sperm.) And above all, use a new condom each time
you have intercourse.

- **Keep a spermicide at the ready,** one that contains Non-
oxynol-9. This kills both sperm and the AIDS virus on
contact.
- **Keep a water-soluble lubricant at the ready.** Oil-based
ones like Vaseline can disintegrate latex on contact.
- **Practice using these** *before* **you have sex,** to get some
proficiency in the mechanics. Try them out at your kitchen
table — and get a friend to join you. This can be fun, and
you can pool your expertise. Use a cucumber or a banana
to stand in for a partner's penis. Practice getting your
giggles out. Then practice putting condoms on, lubricating
them and taking them off. This way, you won't have to
fumble around embarrassingly in the middle of a tender
moment in bed or skip the whole thing at the moment of
intercourse as being just too weird and cumbersome.
- **Learn to eroticize condoms.** How many ways can you
put a condom on? How many kinds of safe lubricant can
you think of? Safer sex can be great sex. Its greatness
improves with practice, but a basic ingredient is your
attitude that sex is good and that sexual experimentation
can be healthy.

4. *Suggest outercourse rather than intercourse.* Remember, AIDS and other STDs are transmitted most efficiently
through intercourse. There are many sexual and sensual activities that are perfectly safe. These include bubblebaths and
massages, romantic dancing, sensuous talking, sensuous eating, sensuous dressing.

5. *Say No if you don't want to have sexual intercourse
or if you have doubts about whether intercourse is safe.*
Top Banana can help you be firm.

6. *Steer clear of drugs and alcohol* — especially in relation
to sex.

7. *Take a realistic view of testing.* By all means, have
yourself and your partner tested if it will give you peace of
mind. And definitely consider testing before getting pregnant.

But testing or no testing, your *safe* bet is to practice the safe-sex Do's outlined above.

If Your Partner Is A Woman

If your partner or potential partner is a woman, you're in a dramatically lower risk group for AIDS or other STDs, and of course unwanted pregnancy is not an issue. But making love with a woman doesn't totally rule out the need for safe sex. If you follow all the steps above (except for condoms), you'll not only stay safe, your sex life should feel clearer, more creative and more satisfying.

If either of you has reason to believe the other might be infected and you feel you must have genital contact, you can wear latex gloves to prevent vaginal fluids from reaching any cuts on your fingers. During oral sex you can use latex squares. They're also known as dental dams and if you can't get them at the drugstore, you can ask your dentist for a bunch — say you're giving a safe-sex lecture if you feel you need an excuse. Latex squares are to spread over the genitals to keep vaginal fluids from entering your mouth.

Detaching With Sex: Doing It Yourself

This book has emphasized women's sexual relationships with partners. But sexuality spans your life from birth to death. No woman has a partner at the ready her whole life long. This doesn't mean that sex has to cease or that sexual recovery has to cease. You have the option of solo sex or, as author Betty Dodson so aptly puts it, *Sex for One.*

This gives you the chance to relate intimately with the most important partner you will ever have — yourself. Consider the following advantages:

- Taking charge of your own sexual enjoyment is entirely safe. You cannot become pregnant by yourself or transmit AIDS or any other STD to yourself.

- Masturbation is a route to enhancing sexual function — and is often the major route to overcoming sexual dysfunction, by familiarizing you with your own responses and rhythms.
  If you're orgasmic, you may make new discoveries about your orgasms. Research indicates that orgasms women give themselves are likely to be deeper, longer, stronger than partner orgasms. Whether or not they are more *satisfying* is a matter of personal preference.
- Masturbating is a superb way to comfort yourself. This way you don't have to be deprived of sexual pleasure if you don't have a partner. Plus, you can keep yourself from sulking when the partner you do have won't or can't come through for you.

Sexual self-pleasure does not always have to be a solo activity. If you have a partner, sharing masturbation can show where and how you like to be touched. When the occasion is right, this degree of sharing can heighten intimacy.

However, self-pleasuring can be fraught with the same kinds of post-traumatic stress, skewed sexual messages and cultural double standard that create sexually co-dependent attitudes and relationships. Fear, guilt, disgust and denial are leftovers from a Victorian age where girls and women who ventured to stimulate themselves were threatened with hellfire and insanity. Beyond psychological bullying, these girls and women were physically violated — by surgical removal of the clitoris or by having their genitals clamped into "chastity" devices studded with metal prongs, like iron maidens.

Aftershocks of these terrors are built into the culture, even today. They continue to spook some women, causing lifelong anguish and causing women to pass along masturbation taboos to their daughters and sons. In the interests of healthy and safe sexuality, it's important to put negativity about masturbation firmly into perspective:

Sexual self-pleasure does not hurt women. What hurts women is misogynistic and sex-negative taboos against self-pleasure.

Imagery And Imagination

Another way to detach with sex is through sexual imagery. Positive sexual fantasy can enhance women's sexual self-esteem and can help heal sexual dysfunction. We've discussed how sexual imagery can help you contact your inner child, deepen your relationship with a partner and even reverse vaginismus.

The full effects of positive imagery on women's sexuality have yet to be researched. What is known is the following:

- Women can and do have sexual fantasies, and these are significant to all phases of their sexual response: desire, arousal and orgasm.
- Women can and do use sexual imagery and fantasy to come to orgasm without any touch.
- Women can and do use sexual imagery and fantasy for sexual control — to regulate the distance from their sexual partners, by bringing them closer or moving them farther away.
- Women can and do use sexual imagery and fantasy to keep their sex lives alive and well during periods of celibacy.

Women can also add excitement to their sexual encounters by sharing their fantasies with their partners. This may require some delicacy and tact if the focus of your fantasy is someone other than your partner. It also requires consummate trust that your partner will not hurt you by using your fantasies against you. This is especially true if your fantasies are of bondage or forced sex — common ones for women.

Sexual imagery can have a dark side for women, dark enough to be toxic. Toxic imagery includes pornography that objectifies and degrades. And it may include women's own fantasies — those fantasies of rape and bondage. While these may be extremely erotic to some women, my clinical experience indicates that they can be disconnecting and eventually erode self-esteem. There's an old saying, beware of what you wish for — because you may get it. The same is true of your sexual fantasies. They may lead to action and strongly affect your life.

This is not to blame you if you're turned on by porn or rape fantasies. You learned this route to sexual excitement directly from the cultural messages you grew up with and perhaps from specific sexual abuses.

It is rather to leave you with the final message of this book: Sexual recovery may involve examining the kinds of imagery that turn you on. It may also involve turning your fantasies around to make them safe.

Imagine yourself as a woman of sexual power, not a recipient of someone else's sexual power. Imagine tenderness instead of pain. See with utmost clarity the flower of sexual renewal blooming up out of the rubble of harassment, violence and fear.

The beginning of lasting sexual change may be here, right in your sexual fantasies. Taking charge of your inner images can strengthen your self-esteem. It can enhance your pleasure. It can encourage you to confront a partner when necessary. Perhaps it can even move you to speak up against the cultural sex-negativity and woman-hating that are at the root of sexual co-dependency for women.

Sexual recovery doesn't mean instant gratification nor does it mean a totally wrinkle-free relationship. Sexual recovery means sexual safety, or at least relative sexual safety, because you are helping to create the conditions that make sex worthwhile.

Sexual recovery moves you toward the freedom to explore your sexual responses, feel your sexual feelings, communicate your desires and hear your partner's desires. And it moves you to enjoy — or think about enjoying — the warm, passionate, loving, intimate pleasure that feeds body, mind, emotions and spirit.

❦ Further Reading About ❦ Women's Sexuality

Allgeier, Elizabeth R. and Albert R. Allgeier. **Sexual Interactions**. Lexington, MA: D.C. Heath and Co., 1984.

A nonsexist textbook that will help answer almost every question you ever wanted to ask about sex.

Barbach, Lonnie G. **For Yourself: The Fulfillment of Female Sexuality**. New York: Anchor/Doubleday, 1976.

The book that has helped thousands of women discover orgasm.

Barbach, Lonnie G. and Linda Levine. **Shared Intimacies: Women's Sexual Experiences**. New York: Bantam Books, 1981.

Women talk about the different ways they make love.

Bell, Ruth, et al. **Changing Bodies, Changing Lives**: Revised Edition. New York: Random House, 1987.

A complete and engaging reference for young women.

Boston Women's Health Collective. **The New Our Bodies, Ourselves**. New York: Simon and Schuster, 1984.

A spirited and indispensible reference on all aspects of women's health, including sexuality.

Bullard, David G. and S. E. Knight. **Sexuality and Physical Disability.** St. Louis: C. V. Mosby, 1981.
An excellent overview of different approaches to sex and disability.

Dodson, Betty. **Sex for One: The Joy of Self-Loving.** New York: Crown, 1987.
The latest book from the woman who liberated women's masturbation.

Hite, Shere. **The Hite Report.** New York: Macmillan, 1976.
The book that first asked women what *they* thought about sex.

Kaplan, Helen S. **The New Sex Therapy.** New York: Bruner/Mazel, 1974.
A clinical guide to dealing with sexual dysfunction.

Kaplan, Helen S. **Disorders of Sexual Desire.** New York: Bruner/Mazel, 1979.
More clinical guidance to sexual function.

Kastl, Charlotte Davis. **Women, Sex, and Addiction: A Search for Love and Power.** New York: Ticknor and Fields, 1989.
How women develop sexual compulsions and addictions.

Kensington Ladies' Erotica Society. **Ladies' Own Erotica.** Berkeley, CA: Ten Speed Press, 1984.
Light-hearted housewives write lighthearted erotica.

Kinsey, Alfred C., Wardell Pomeroy, Clyde Martin and Paul Gebhard. **Sexual Behavior in the Human Female.** Philadelphia: W.B. Saunders, 1953.
The research that helped America out of the Victorian dark ages of sexual myth and misinformation.

Klausner, Mary Ann, and Bobbie Hasselbring. **Aching for Love: The Sexual Drama of the Adult Child.** San Francisco: Harper & Row, 1990.
A well-documented overview of why ACoAs develop sexual problems.

Ladas, Alice K., Beverly Whipple and John D. Perry. **The G Spot and Other Recent Discoveries about Human Sexuality.** New York: Holt, Rinehart and Winston, 1982.
A new theory of orgasm for women.

Loulan, JoAnn. **Lesbian Sex.** San Francisco: Spinsters Ink, 1987. A down-to earth look at how women make love with women.

Loulan, JoAnn. **Lesbian Passion.** San Francisco: Spinsters Ink, 1987.
More news about lesbian sexuality.

Masters, William H. and Virginia E. Johnson. **Human Sexual Response.** Boston: Little, Brown, 1966.
The landmark studies of women's and men's sexual response.

Thornton, Louise, Jan Sturtevant and Amber Coverdale Sumrall. **Touching Fire: Erotic Writings by Women.** New York: Carroll and Graf, 1989.
Gentle, spiritual erotica, by and for women.

Whipple, Beverly and Gina Ogden. **Safe Encounters: How Women Can Say Yes to Pleasure and No to Unsafe Sex.** New York: McGraw-Hill, 1989 (Pocket Books, 1990).
Positive, explicit guidance for women in the age of AIDS.

Zilbergeld, Bernie. **Male Sexuality.** New York: Bantam, 1978.
For your male partner.

❦ Resources For Information ❦ About Sexuality

American Association of Sex Educators, Counselors and Therapists (AASECT)

Eleven Dupont Circle N.W.
Suite 220
Washington, DC 20036
202-462-1171

Certifying organization for sexuality professionals all over the country. AASECT can refer you to a trained sex counselor or therapist in your area.

National AIDS Hotline

800-342-2437

Information on testing, support groups, referrals. Someone is there to answer questions about AIDS 24 hours a day, seven days a week.

Planned Parenthood of America
810 7th Avenue
New York, NY 10019
800-223-3303
212-541-7800
(or call your local chapter)

For information on all aspects of reproductive health.

Sex Information and Education Council of the United States (SIECUS)
32 Washington Place
New York, NY 10003

Can guide you to books, articles, tapes and films on all aspects of sexuality.

Victims of Incest Can Emerge (VOICE)
Voices in Action, Inc.
P.O. Box 148309
Chicago, IL 60614
312-327-1500

Can refer you to therapists, agencies and self-help groups recommended by survivors.

INDEX

Other Books By . . .
Health Communications

ADULT CHILDREN OF ALCOHOLICS
Janet Woititz
Over a year on *The New York Times* Best-Seller list, this book is the primer on Adult Children of Alcoholics.
ISBN 0-932194-15-X $6.95

STRUGGLE FOR INTIMACY
Janet Woititz
Another best-seller, this book gives insightful advice on learning to love more fully.
ISBN 0-932194-25-7 $6.95

BRADSHAW ON: THE FAMILY: A Revolutionary Way of Self-Discovery
John Bradshaw
The host of the nationally televised series of the same name shows us how families can be healed and individuals can realize full potential.
ISBN 0-932194-54-0 $9.95

HEALING THE SHAME THAT BINDS YOU
John Bradshaw
This important book shows how toxic shame is the core problem in our compulsions and offers new techniques of recovery vital to all of us.
ISBN 0-932194-86-9 $9.95

*HEALING THE CHILD WITHIN: Discovery and Recovery for
Adult Children of Dysfunctional Families* — Charles Whitfield, M.D.
Dr. Whitfield defines, describes and discovers how we can reach our Child Within to heal and nurture our woundedness.
ISBN 0-932194-40-0 $8.95

A GIFT TO MYSELF: A Personal Guide To Healing My Child Within
Charles L. Whitfield, M.D.
Dr. Whitfield provides practical guidelines and methods to work through the pain and confusion of being an Adult Child of a dysfunctional family.
ISBN 1-55874-042-2 $11.95

*HEALING TOGETHER: A Guide To Intimacy And Recovery For
Co-dependent Couples* — Wayne Kritsberg, M.A.
This is a practical book that tells the reader why he or she gets into dysfunctional and painful relationships, and then gives a concrete course of action on how to move the relationship toward health.
ISBN 1-55784-053-8 $8.95

3201 S.W. 15th Street,
Deerfield Beach, FL 33442
1-800-851-9100

**Health
Communications, Inc.**

Books from . . .
Health Communications

PERFECT DAUGHTERS: Adult Daughters Of Alcoholics
Robert Ackerman
Through a combined narrative of professional and anecdotal styles Robert
Ackerman helps restore a sense of balance in life for Adult Daughters of
Alcoholics.
ISBN 1-55874-040-6 **$8.95**

I DON'T WANT TO BE ALONE:
For Men And Women Who Want To Heal Addictive Relationships
John Lee
John Lee describes the problems of co-dependent relationships and his
realization that he may be staying in such a relationship because of his
fear of being alone.
ISBN 1-55874-065-1 **$8.95**

SHAME AND GUILT: Masters Of Disguise
Jane Middelton-Moz
The author uses myths and fairy tales to portray different shaming
environments and to show how shame can keep you from being the
person you were born to be.
ISBN 1-55874-072-4 **$8.95**

LIFESKILLS FOR ADULT CHILDREN
Janet G. Woititz and Alan Garner
This book teaches you the interpersonal skills that can make your life easier
while improving your sense of self-worth. Examples are provided to help
clarify the lessons and exercises are given for practicing your new skills.
ISBN 1-55874-070-8 **$8.95**

THE MIRACLE OF RECOVERY:
Healing For Addicts, Adult Children And Co-dependents
Sharon Wegscheider-Cruse
This is about the good news — that recovery from co-dependency is
possible. Sharon offers ways to embrace the positive aspects of one's
experience — to realize the strength that can come from adversity.
Celebrate your own miracle with this inspiring book.
ISBN 1-55874-024-4 **$9.95**

SHIPPING/HANDLING: All orders shipped UPS unless weight exceeds 200 lbs., special routing is requested, or
delivery territory is outside continental U.S. Orders outside United States shipped either Air Parcel Post or Surface
Parcel Post. Shipping and handling charges apply to all orders shipped whether UPS, Book Rate, Library Rate, Air
or Surface Parcel Post or Common Carrier and will be charged as follows. Orders less than $25.00 in value add
$2.00 minimum. Orders from $25.00 to $50.00 in value (after discount) add $2.50 minimum. Orders greater than
$50.00 in value (after discount) add 6% of value. Orders greater than $25.00 outside United States add 15% of
value. We are not responsible for loss or damage unless material is shipped UPS. Allow 3-5 weeks after receipt of
order for delivery. Prices are subject to change without prior notice.

3201 S.W. 15th Street,
Deerfield Beach, FL 33442-8124
1-800-851-9100

Health
Communications, Inc.